Decolonial Love in Times of Hatred

Decolonial Love in Times of Hatred

Forty Ways to Follow Jesus Today

OSCAR GARCÍA-JOHNSON

CASCADE *Books* • Eugene, Oregon

DECOLONIAL LOVE IN TIMES OF HATRED
Forty Ways to Follow Jesus Today

Copyright © 2026 Oscar García-Johnson. All rights reserved. Except for brief quotations in critical publications or reviews, no part of this book may be reproduced in any manner without prior written permission from the publisher. Write: Permissions, Wipf and Stock Publishers, 199 W. 8th Ave., Suite 3, Eugene, OR 97401.

Cascade Books
An Imprint of Wipf and Stock Publishers
199 W. 8th Ave., Suite 3
Eugene, OR 97401

www.wipfandstock.com

PAPERBACK ISBN: 979-8-3852-4186-6
HARDCOVER ISBN: 979-8-3852-4187-3
EBOOK ISBN: 979-8-3852-4188-0

Cataloguing-in-Publication data:

Names: García-Johnson, Oscar [author].

Title: Decolonial love in times of hatred : forty ways to follow Jesus / by Oscar García-Johnson.

Description: Eugene, OR: Cascade Books, 2026 | Includes bibliographical references.

Identifiers: ISBN 979-8-3852-4186-6 (paperback) | ISBN 979-8-3852-4187-3 (hardcover) | ISBN 979-8-3852-4188-0 (ebook)

Subjects: LCSH: Christian life. | Spiritual formation. | Christianity—21st century. | Church renewal.

Classification: BV4501.3 G37 2026 (paperback) | BV4501.3 (ebook)

VERSION NUMBER 01/29/26

To the cloud of witnesses that feel displaced by an unusual era of hatred, fragmentation, and enmity and feel the call to go all the way with our Lord.

> *For in seven days' time I will make it rain upon the earth*
> *for forty days and forty nights,*
> *and I will blot out from the earth all existence that I created.*
>
> —Genesis 7:4 from *The Contemporary Torah*

> *Jesus, full of the Holy Spirit,*
> *returned from the Jordan and was led by the Spirit in the wilderness,*
> *where forty days he was tempted by the devil.*
> *He ate nothing at all during those days, and*
> *when they were over, he was*
> *famished.* . . .
> *Jesus, filled with the power of the Spirit, returned to Galilee,*
> *and a report about him spread through all the surrounding country.*
>
> —Luke 4:1–2, 14

> *After he had suffered by being put to death on the cross,*
> *he returned to life and then appeared to his message bearers,*
> *giving them many proofs that he was truly alive again.*
> *For forty days he continued to appear to them,*
> *and through the Holy Spirit he instructed them*
> *further about Creator's good road.*
>
> —Acts 1:3 FNV

Contents

Acknowledgments | xi
Abbreviations | xiii
Introduction | xv

Day 1
Loneliness, Hatred, and Healing | 1

Day 2
World Disappointments | 4

Day 3
Fear of God | 9

Day 4
Self-Denial | 13

Day 5
Renunciation: The Preferential Option for Jesus | 18

Day 6
Charity in a World of Philanthropists | 23

Day 7
Cleansing of Character and Spiritual Freedom | 29

Day 8
Moderation | 34

Day 9
Holiness: So Human, It Can Only Be Godly | 39

Contents

Day 10
Liberation: From Letters in Red to Works in Red | 44

Day 11
Divine Order | 50

Day 12
Vision and Vocation | 55

Day 13
Social Responsibility: Becoming A Public Witness | 60

Day 14
The Social Bubble | 66

Day 15
Secrets | 72

Day 16
Aspirations | 76

Day 17
Conviviality: A Probiotic Theology | 80

Day 18
Temptation | 85

Day 19
Words of Life and Words of Death | 89

Day 20
Mother | 94

Day 21
Abba Father and Social Orphanhood | 98

Day 22
Tomorrow | 103

Day 23
Gratitude: Grace as an Alternative to Meanness | 108

Day 24
Redemption and Abandonment | 112

Day 25
Devotional Life: Starting the Day with Sacred Intention | 117

Contents

Day 26
Righteous Compassion | 122

Day 27
Stumbling in Perseverance | 127

Day 28
Obedient Leadership | 131

Day 29
Intimacy with God: Believing *Where* We Are | 135

Day 30
Trust | 140

Day 31
Comfort | 145

Day 32
Sensuous Reason (*Sentipensar*) | 150

Day 33
Obsession | 154

Day 34
Poor in Spirit | 159

Day 35
Justice | 164

Day 36
Peace | 168

Day 37
Testimony: *Auto-Historia* as Spiritual Activism | 173

Day 38
The Power of God | 178

Day 39
Service as Christopraxis | 184

Day 40
The Last and Wretched of the World | 189

Epilogue: From Half-Way to All-the-Way Discipleship | 195
Endnotes | 199
Bibliography | 203

Acknowledgments

DECOLONIAL LOVE IN TIMES OF HATRED represents a sort of bornagain text. Its predecessor, *Jesús, hazme como tú* (2010), was written in Spanish for a popular audience as a collection of reflections for Lent. The current iteration is not a linguistic translation so much as it is an intercultural, interpolitical, and sociohistorical one. Without the first life of this text, it would have been impossible to produce the second life as you have it. Thanks to the following:

Karen Hamilton Lucas, my research assistant, who assisted with style.

My wife who, as usual, generated the ecology for praying, thinking, and writing at home.

My students and allies from the Fuller Student Group: Decolonial Conversations, for their creative and challenging engagement.

Wipf and Stock Publishers and, especially, Michael Thomson who believed in this project and made it possible to produce this book in a timely manner for such a time like ours.

Scripture Abbreviations

THIS DEVOTIONAL USES MULTIPLE translations of the Bible, the abbreviations and copyright statements for which are below. Italics have been added by the author.

Scripture quotations are from the New Revised Standard Version, copyright © 1989 National Council of Churches of Christ in the United States of America. Used by Permission. All rights reserved.

Scripture quotations marked CEB are from the Common English Bible, copyright © 2011 Common English Bible. All rights reserved. Used by permission. www.commonenglishbible.com

Scripture quotations marked CJB are from the Complete Jewish Bible, copyright © 1998 by David H. Stearn. Published by Jewish New Testament Publications, Inc. Distributed by Messianic Jewish Resources Int'l. All rights reserved. Used by permission. www.messianicjewish.net.

Scripture quotations marked ESV are from The Holy Bible, English Standard Version®, copyright 2001 by Crossway, a publishing ministry of Good News Publishers. Used by permission.

Scripture quotations marked FNV are from *First Nations Version: An Indigenous Translation of the New Testament*, copyright © 2021

Scripture Abbreviations

by Rain Ministries, Inc. Used by permission of InterVarsity Press. All rights reserved worldwide. www.ivpress.com.

Scripture quotations marked NIV are from The Holy Bible, New International Version®, NIV®, copyright © 1973, 1978, 1984, 2014 by Biblica, Inc. Used with permission of Zondervan. www.zondervan.com

Scripture quotations marked NRSVue are taken from the New Revised Standard Version Updated Edition, copyright © 2021 National Council of Churches of Christ in the United States of America. Used by permission. All rights reserved worldwide.

Introduction

WE LIVE IN A moment of profound division—not only within societies but also within the body of Christ worldwide. Over the past decade, US American Christianity has often appeared fragmented, politicized, and diminished by cultural hatred and ideological entrenchment. For many, faith has been co-opted into a tool of cultural warfare or a patriotic narrative that obscures the radical love of Jesus Christ. Yet, amid the noise, the call of Jesus remains as urgent as ever: to embody his love, humility, and justice in a world fractured by hostility, a radical act of obedience—*imitatio Christi*.

In such a time as ours, after more than five centuries of Christian presence on this continent, an irrepressible question remains: What should be the shape of the Christian witness capable of addressing the most pressing threats of our time?

In 1957, the literary world was surprised by the nomination of a relatively young writer from Algeria for the Nobel Prize in Literature: Albert Camus. A member of the North African Resistance and hailing from poverty-stricken origins, Camus received the prize alongside a commendation from the secretary of the Swedish Academy, marked by the subtlety of Eurocentric pedantry:

> French literature is no longer linked geographically to the frontiers of France in Europe. In many respects, it reminds one of a garden plant, noble and irreplaceable, which, when cultivated outside its territory, still retains its distinctive character, although tradition and variation

Introduction

alternately influence it. The Nobel Laureate for this year, Albert Camus, is an example of this evolution.¹

At the Nobel Prize Banquet in Stockholm on December 10, 1957, Camus revealed to his audience the character and vision of a young writer committed to humility, gratitude, solidarity with those who suffer injustice, and the struggle for human dignity and political freedom. His speech also reflected his painful artistic vocation as a voice for truth and liberty in oppressive times. One of his most memorable passages, worth quoting at length, underscores his generational ethos:

> Each generation doubtless feels called upon to reform the world. Mine knows that it will not reform it, but its task is perhaps even greater. It consists in preventing the world from destroying itself. Heir to a corrupt history, in which are mingled fallen revolutions, technology gone mad, dead gods, and worn-out ideologies—where mediocre powers can destroy all yet no longer know how to convince, where intelligence has debased itself to become the servant of hatred and oppression—this generation, starting from its own negations, has had to re-establish, both within and without, a little of that which constitutes the dignity of life and death. In a world threatened by disintegration, in which our grand inquisitors risk establishing forever the kingdom of death, it knows that it should, in an insane race against the clock, restore among the nations a peace that is not servitude, reconcile anew labor and culture, and remake with all men the Ark of the Covenant. It is not certain that this generation will ever be able to accomplish this immense task, but already it is rising everywhere in the world to the double challenge of truth and liberty and, if necessary, knows how to die for it without hate.²

What Has Actually Changed?

As a US citizen of Honduran origins living in Southern California during a time of strategic wars, intense political polarization, unprecedented populist fascism, post-pandemic consumerism, growing immigration terror, and spreading religious hatred, I am struck by the parallels between Camus's generation and mine. Whatever has changed in the last seven decades seems to have only heightened humanity's capacity for sophisticated oppression and concealed hatred.

On the flip side of historical pessimism, however, I feel inspired by Camus's sense of generational vocation, particularly with respect to:

1. Serving others as best I can with the tools I possess.
2. Remaining vigilant against injustice while advocating for freedom and dignity, starting with the most vulnerable.
3. Teaching and writing to inspire hope amid despair and godly fear amid violent triumphalism.
4. Engaging in the task of *re-existing*—remaking the world by first remaking ourselves.

Evidently, I am not the most qualified candidate to follow in Camus's footsteps. For that, we had Gabriel García Márquez, one of my literary heroes and another Nobel Laureate in Literature (1982). Influenced by Camus during his formative years, García Márquez's novel *Love in the Time of Cholera* captured my attention some years ago. There was something about the title and its metaphorical correspondence between love and illness in the Americas that stuck with me.

Human Love—A Fiction We Embrace as Illness or Healing

Love, a premier theological leitmotif in both conservative and progressive Christian traditions, is portrayed with ambivalence in *Love in the Time of Cholera*. Like a disease, love destabilizes and consumes individuals with passion, obsession, and irrationality—but also with vitality and hope. Similarly, *cholera*, set in nineteenth-century Latin America, symbolizes societal decay, evoking

INTRODUCTION

colonial legacies, ethno-racial-gender hierarchies, and political corruption. Yet love persists—healing love and wounding love.

Latin Americans, like many marginalized communities, develop resilience through love and because of love. Love emerges vividly amid struggle, giving meaning in hopelessness and magical imagination in the form of healing fictions of timeless love and historical renewal. It is against the backdrop of a diseased social imagination—infecting families, churches, economies, and political structures—that this collection of Lent reflections is set.

Decolonial Love in Times of Hatred

This collection, *Decolonial Love in Times of Hatred*, offers an alternative to the shallow discipleship that aligns faith with power, privilege, and division. It invites us to remember, re-emerge, and reimagine resilient Christian love energized by the gospel as a better way to live together amid social illness and the plague of hatred.

Decolonial Love in Times of Hatred is not a maximum-utopian vision to remake the world systems at once but a *teotopian* invitation to take one step at a time from within the cracks and fissures of oppressive landscapes. We could only do this as disciples shaped by the Spirit, not culture wars; by the cross, not the flag; and by God's kingdom, not political empires. It is a call to *all-the-way discipleship*,[3] transcending the half-hearted models of faith possessed by the ideologies of our age.

The early-Christian desert fathers and mothers abandoned the comforts of their age to confront their sinfulness and encounter God in the wilderness. Today, we do not need to physically enter a desert; the desert has come to us. The isolation, temptation, and fragmentation of modern life have invaded our cities, suburbs, and sanctuaries. The ferocity of hyper-individualism, consumerism, and anxiety has turned our daily environments into inhospitable deserts for the self.

Yet, just as the desert became a place of transformation for early Christians, our current wilderness offers an opportunity. The spiritual disciplines of solitude, simplicity, humility, and radical

INTRODUCTION

obedience practiced by the desert Christians may seem alien to our pursuit of personal success and the American dream, but they hold the key to reclaiming the radical obedience that marked their lives. This book challenges us to embrace a discipleship of decolonial love—a life that rejects the idols of materialism, cultural power, racial privilege, and dogmatic division and instead seeks to embody Jesus Christ in the desert of our time.

From Devotional to Missional: A Journey of Transformation

The forty reflections in this collection are not systematic theology or classical spirituality; they are deeply personal meditations born of everyday struggles and inspired by Scripture, history, and the Spirit. They emerged from a season of imagining myself soul-bare before the risen Christ, seeking to live the teachings of his kingdom amid the world's brokenness. In a sense, these forty reflections are my *confessions* of faith expressed in the public sphere, with fear and trembling. They are not intended as universal propositions of *what* to believe or do but as an invitation to believe together *where* we experience suffering, anxiety, oppression, injustice, beauty, hope, worship, and integral transformation.

Each entry reflects the tension between longing for divine transformation and grappling with the realities of daily life. Borrowing from Gloria Anzaldúa's *autohistoria-teoría*, this journey invites us to reshape our personal and collective stories around the liberating, justice-oriented love of Jesus.[4] Through these reflections, you are invited into a process of surrender—forty days of fasting from your will to align yourself with the will of God.

They can be used devotionally, accompanied by journaling and prayer; missionally, as a framework for living out the gospel in your community; and pedagogically, as a resource for teaching and discussion. All together, these forty entries anticipate a season of change. You may dedicate fifteen to twenty minutes each day to read, reflect, and write. But do not stop there. Allow these reflections to guide a lifelong pursuit of Christ, embodying his love and justice in every moment, in every place, in every community.

Let us begin!

Endnotes

1. Österling, "Award Ceremony Speech."
2. Camus, "Albert Camus—Banquet Speech."
3. "All-the-way-discipleship" is a phrase inspired by Meister Eckhart, who said, "There are plenty to follow our Lord half-way, but not the other half. They will give up possessions, friends and honors, but it touches them too closely to disown themselves." Eckhart, quoted in Kelly, *Testament of Devotion*, 52.
4. Anzaldúa, *Borderlands*.

Day 1

Loneliness, Hatred, and Healing

Scripture

Then the Lord God said, "It's not good that the human is alone."

—Genesis 2:18 CEB

Now when Jesus heard this, he withdrew from there in a boat to a deserted place by himself.

—Matthew 14:13

The Depth of Loneliness and Hatred

WE ALL NEED EMOTIONAL health to be happy. Loneliness is a symptom of unhappiness. US American evangelist Billy Graham once noted that North Americans were feeling lonelier than ever, despite being surrounded by wealth, commodities, and the freedom of religion.[1] This observation has kept me pondering for decades.

What deepened my understanding of loneliness and hatred was reading Fr. Bartolomé de Las Casas's *A Brief Account of the*

Destruction of the Indies. Las Casas's 1552 vivid portrayal of the colonial atrocities committed against Indigenous populations—and the same can be applied to enslaved African communities and women during colonial times—reveals a painful history of systemic hatred and dehumanization. How could Christian missions have participated in the genocidal and violent extermination of entire populations and the erasure of their cultural origins? Howard Thurman, in his reflection on the "anatomy of hatred," articulates a powerful insight into the cyclical nature of human emotions: "Love begets love, hate begets hate, and indifference begets indifference."[2]

Our society often ties health to superficial attributes, neglecting deep emotional and spiritual wellness. True health encompasses our connections with others, aligning with God's declaration, "It's not good that the human is alone." Despite my upbringing, which taught me to connect with others empathetically, I have become lonelier in a modern Western society that struggles to form deep, empathetic relationships.

Businesses today are dedicated to helping us make friends and find dates, while media platforms amplify anger and hate toward opponents. Yet, loneliness remains a burden that contradicts our created nature. Biblical texts remind us that living in isolation leads to unhappiness, which can culminate in spiritual and physical death.

The Healing Power of Community

In the narrative of Jesus, we find hope. Jesus embraced our humanity and demonstrated the importance of community through his life. The apostle Paul urges us to put away our old selves and clothe ourselves with the new self, created in the likeness of God in Christ Jesus (Eph 3:10; 4:22, 24). This new self thrives in companionship with others, hence "righteous and holy."

Christian tradition includes the discipline of solitude, seeking to be alone for spiritual renewal. Henri Nouwen observed that true solitude is transformative, allowing our old selves to die and new selves to be born.[3] Dietrich Bonhoeffer emphasized the balance between solitude and community: "Let him who cannot be alone beware of community. . . . Let him who is not in community beware of being alone."[4]

Centering Thought

In Christ, we find the courage to face loneliness and the grace to transform it into connection. Through authentic relationships, grounded in God's Spirit, we heal wounds of hatred and indifference, becoming agents of renewal in a fragmented world. Solitude with God empowers us for community, and in community, we embody the fullness of God's love.

Prayer

Jesus, make me like you!
Liberate me from the sinful colonial hatred.
Help me to see your image in every person I encounter,
To love with sincerity, and to build bridges where hatred seeks to divide.
Teach me to embrace the solitude that renews my spirit,
So that I may embody your love in a world longing for connection.
Amen.

Personal Journal Prompts

- Dedicate one hour to be in solitude, in silence and alone.
- Think about the moments when you have felt most alone. Write down whatever comes to mind.
- Do you feel God more deeply when alone or with others?
- Are there certain people who make you feel God's presence more or less? How do you navigate this?
- What do you see in Jesus that teaches you to be in solitude in order to be in community, and in community to be in solitude?

Day 2

World Disappointments

Scripture

*"Where are you?" He answered,
"I heard you in the garden, and I was afraid
because I was naked; so I hid."
And he said, "Who told you that you were naked?"*

—Genesis 3:9–11 NIV

What Is Disappointment All About?

WE ARE CREATORS AND dreamers by nature. We thrive on hope, building aspirations around people and circumstances in search of happiness. Yet, disappointment is an inevitable part of this process. In English, the word "illusion" often implies deception, while its Latin root includes also a sense of playfulness. In Spanish, *ilusión* embodies the hopeful playfulness of dreaming about a better life or experience. Our aspirations—*ilusiones*—are among the most beautiful expressions of our humanity, but they come with a price.

When our hopes are grounded in authentic relationships or true encounters with life, they often flourish into reality. However, when based on deception, they form a false sense of security that is eventually unmasked, leaving us disillusioned. Disappointment arises when false hopes confront the truth. For example, I discovered how deeply Latin American and Welsh I was only after migrating to the United States and becoming part of the Latino/a diaspora. Similarly, the people of biblical Israel discovered their Jewish identity during exile. This principle holds across all areas of life: family, work, ministry, love, art, and more.

Our initial reaction to disappointment is often denial. We cling to illusions, sometimes blaming others for our disillusionment—calling them liars, deceivers, or opportunists. But genuine growth requires personal courage, honesty, and the support of healing communities to transform disappointment into opportunities for flourishing. Adam and Eve's transition out of Eden into maturity in Gen 3 illustrates this well.

Identifying Modern Sources of Deception

Living truthfully involves acknowledging the interconnectedness of our bodies, other living beings, and the world around us. Unfortunately, Western modernity, influenced by Enlightenment thinkers like René Descartes and Isaac Newton, often separates knowledge from embodiment. This Cartesian dualism elevated rational thought above physical and sensory experiences, laying the foundation for modern scientific, theological, and economic systems.

While Enlightenment ideas enabled remarkable progress for the West, they also led to a disembodied worldview for the rest. Nature became a resource to be exploited, fostering environmental degradation and social alienation. This mechanistic perspective prioritized individualism and intellectualism at the expense of communal and ecological well-being. As a result, we live under illusions of disembodied knowledge, disconnected relationships, and false visions of the future, perpetually cycling through disappointment. We have become acutely aware of this at the beginning of the twenty-first century, as wars around the world have erupted, a global pandemic shook the world, genocides have loomed as inevitable, and political polarization have permeated daily life.

Embracing Indigenous Sources of Healing

Indigenous communities around the world have resisted this disconnection, preserving holistic ways of living that emphasize embodied wisdom and deep ties to land, ancestors, and ecosystems. Western modernity often dismissed these practices as "backward," but they offer profound insights for healing and living truthfully.

One example is *Buen Vivir*, or "Good Living," a concept from Andean Indigenous traditions. It emphasizes harmony with nature, community well-being, and a balanced integration of physical, emotional, spiritual, and social dimensions. *Buen Vivir* advocates sustainable living, responsible resource management, and a respect for Mother Earth (*Pachamama*). By fostering interconnectedness, it challenges the exploitative tendencies of global capitalism and offers an alternative path to true flourishing.

Living Truly

Buen Vivir inspires an embodied way of living that aligns with truth and well-being. It presents a holistic and sustainable alternative to the disembodied and exploitative practices of modern life. By integrating respect for nature, communal solidarity, and holistic well-being, it embodies the principle that "another world is possible."[5] God's truth calls us to unmask false hopes and illusions. Disappointment, though painful, can be a divine gift that draws us closer to reality and away from deception. Indigenous wisdom, while often marginalized, carries elements of God's healing presence, guiding us to live authentically and embrace God's love as expressed in creation and community.

Jesus Christ is the ultimate embodiment of truth and faithfulness. This is not meant as a dogmatic statement. One does not need to convert to Christianity to benefit from what Jesus Christ offers. This idea may seem shocking to some, yet there is biblical precedent to suggest that some may fulfill Jesus's teachings and practices outside the orthodox framework of Christianity (Luke 9:49–50). For example, the Hindu leader Mahatma Gandhi admired Jesus Christ and embraced the Sermon on the Mount daily, yet he criticized Jesus's followers for failing to fully embody his teachings and practices. Similarly, figures like Rabbi Abraham Heschel, the Dalai Lama (Tenzin Gyatso), Vietnamese Zen Buddhist Thich Nhat Hanh, and Indian poet and reformer Rabindranath Tagore all connected with Jesus's vision of life, justice, and compassion, while remaining distanced from the institutionalized form of Christianity in modern times.

Centering Thought

Jesus's embodied and resurgent truth precedes and transcends the Christian religion. His declaration as "the way, the truth, and the life" provides a path to God, calling us to foster mature, authentic relationships with one another and with creation. Jesus's life, death, and resurrection reveal the triumph of truth over deception. The cross, as the embodiment of decolonial love against *Pax Romana*, redeems unjust suffering and directs us toward *shalom*. Jesus models an authentic way of living, rooted in harmony with creation and grounded in ecological and communal redemption.

Prayer

Jesus, help me heal from the devastating effects of disappointment.
Guide me toward maturity and the fullness of life.
Jesus, make me like you!
Make me someone who lives authentically,
embracing Good Living and building others up,
even beyond Christian boundaries, yet never apart from you!

Personal Journal Prompts

- Recall a disappointment you've experienced. How did you respond, and what helped you move forward?
- How do you connect with nature and your community? What practices help you foster harmony in these relationships?
- How does Jesus's example challenge or inspire you? What steps can you take to live more authentically, moving away from illusions and false hopes?

Day 3

Fear of God

Scripture

*In this world we are like Jesus. In love there is no fear. . . .
For the love of God is this, that we obey his commandments.*

—1 JOHN 4:17–18 NIV; 1 JOHN 5:3

The Nature of Godless Fear and Godly Love

TO LIVE FULLY AND joyfully, we all need love. Yet love's greatest enemy is not hatred but godless fear or terror. Fear, in itself, is not bad but fear without God is a pathology of hatred, as we have noted in day 1. Godless fear often emerges from loneliness, ignorance, false hope, insecurity, and, most profoundly, abusive love. It is the antithesis of trust, connection, and intimacy.

We will never fully love whom we dread, and we will never dread whom we fully love. Love cannot grow in the soil of godless fear and terror; the two cannot coexist. Scripture presents two complementary truths that help us understand this paradox:

1. **We shall love God, for God is love** (Exod 34:6–7; Deut 6:5; Matt 22:37–38; 1 John 4:7–8).

2. **We shall fear God, for God is just and holy** (Prov 9:10; Isa 6:3–5; Luke 22:4–5; Rev 15:4).

At first glance, these teachings seem contradictory, but they come together in a profound way. The *fear of God* is not a terror of divine wrath that punishes every mistake without compassion. Instead, the fear of God refers to a profound awareness of God's presence in every moment and aspect of our lives. It is the awe-filled recognition of God's majesty, love, and justice that compels us to surrender and obey knowing that God is our ultimate good, our *Summum Bonum*. This holy fear brings us closer to God by grounding us in humility and reverence, anticipating intimacy. We fear hurting or distancing from whom we fully love.

Fear of God: A Path to Love

We learn to love God fully when we recognize God's omnipresence and respond with surrender and obedience. This surrender is not subjugation but an act of trust and intimacy. True love for God matures as we align our lives with God's will. God's will shall never be confused with our own will. It is an embrace, a *perichoresis* of righteous love and godly fear between different beings.

Jesus Christ is the fullest manifestation of God's love among us. In Jesus, we encounter a God who is not distant and punitive but compassionate, tender, and sacrificial. Jesus teaches us to love even those we find hardest to love—our enemies and those who seek our harm. This radical love demonstrates the true nature of fearing God: trusting God so completely that we align ourselves with God's action in the world, even when it leads to suffering or shame. Cruciformity is the shape of this radical love and godly fear, a public Christian witness that unmasks the true nature of imperial, corporate, religious, or domestic violence as abusive love or godless fear.

To fear God, as modeled by Jesus, is to live in courageous obedience to God's will, knowing that radical love overcomes godless fear. This obedience often runs counter to the colonial narratives of domination and exclusion naturalized today by many institutional operations (law and order) and political ideologies (right and left) shaping our modern theologies and cultures. Instead, it calls us to embrace a decolonial love—one that dismantles systems of hatred, fear, and oppression by embodying God's justice and compassion in cruciformity.

Decolonial Love and Fear of God

In a world marred by colonial legacies of terror—fear of the other, fear of difference, fear of vulnerability—the fear of God redirects us toward love. Decolonial love, a term rooted in the work of intellectuals like Frantz Fanon and bell hooks, challenges us to unlearn oppressive patterns and embrace radical interdependence.[6] It is a love that resists the forces of hatred and exclusion by affirming the dignity and humanity of all and its inescapable covenant with creation as an act of fearing God.

To fear God in this context means to stand against systems that perpetuate violence and exploitation. It requires us to acknowledge the divine image in every person, especially those marginalized by society. This holy fear transforms us into agents of healing, justice, and reconciliation.

As Jesus demonstrated, fearing God often comes with a cost. It may demand that we confront hatred with love, endure suffering for the sake of justice, or relinquish our comfort to serve others. Yet, in this surrender, we discover the profound blessing of living in alignment with God's will—a life marked by *shalom*, the peace and wholeness that reflects God's kingdom.

Living the Fear of God

To fear God is to trust fully in God's radical love and justice. It is to stand in awe of God's presence while aligning our lives with God's mission of reconciliation and renewal. This alignment does not foster dread but liberates us to live authentically and courageously.

Through Jesus Christ, we are invited to embody this holy fear in our relationships and communities. It challenges us to build bridges where fear creates walls, to seek justice where hatred thrives, and to pursue communion through peace in a world fractured by division.

Centering Thought

By surrendering to God's will and embodying decolonial love, we join Jesus in the redemptive work of building a world where godly fear overcomes imperial terror and leads to love and *shalom*.

Prayer

Jesus, deliver me from the chains of terror,
Guide me onto the path of radical love.
Free me from the roots of violence against my opponents.
Jesus, make me like you!
Make me a person who fears God,
living in awe and surrender,
embodying cruciform love in a world consumed by hatred.

Personal Journal Prompts

- What do you most fear? Now, put a face on it! What do you most love in life? Put a face on that too! How are these connected?
- How difficult is it for you to bless those who have wronged you or may wrong you? Reflect on ways you can embody Jesus's radical love.
- How can you grow in trusting and fearing God, rather than the other? What steps can you take to align your will with Jesus's radical way of loving the enemy?

Day 4

Self-Denial

Scripture

Whoever does not carry their cross and follow me cannot be my disciple. If anyone comes to me and does not sacrifice love for father and mother, wife and children, brothers and sisters—yes, even their own life—they cannot be my disciple.

—Luke 14:27–28 NIV

Self-Denial: The Fasting of the Ego

TRUE HAPPINESS AND FULFILLMENT require self-denial, which can be understood as the fasting of the addition of the *self*. When we indulge every desire without restraint, we become slaves to the excesses of the ego. Self-centeredness, or "ego-logy," is a way of living that places the self at the center of all things. This mindset gives rise to selfishness (egoism) and self-worship (egolatry), which are like unruly twins dwelling within the house of an ego-driven person.

Living under the domination of the ego is akin to worshiping an idol we have placed within ourselves. This idolatry damages our relationship with the Creator and reduces our connections with others to manipulative and transactional interactions. The cure for this condition is self-denial—a deliberate rejection of the false self in order to uncover and recover the true self.

Self-denial is a journey inward, where we confront the fantasies of the ego and liberate a mind ensnared by selfishness and self-worship. God created us as relational beings, intended to live, not in isolation or self-reference but in communion with *the other*. This other includes God, our human neighbors, and the entire created world. Egoism, egocentrism, and egolatry are symptoms of a deeper problem: living as though we are the center of the universe, and in doing so, positioning ourselves as adversaries of God and others.

Ego-logy: The Philosophy of Self-Worship

The term "ego-logy" reflects the philosophical tendency to exalt the self above all else. Philosophers such as Friedrich Nietzsche and Ayn Rand emphasized individualism and self-determination as the highest values, promoting a worldview in which the individual's desires and achievements are paramount.[7] While these ideas challenge oppressive collectivism, they also foster a culture of self-idolatry and unchecked ambition.

Ego-logy teaches us to view the self as autonomous and detached from relationships, prioritizing personal goals over communal well-being. This mindset feeds into systems of exploitation, consumerism, and environmental degradation, all of which are rooted in the belief that the world exists to serve individual desires and the strongest will wins. It creates an illusion of independence while fostering alienation from God, others, and creation.

Self-Indulgence and Narcissism: The Psychological Trap

Behavioral psychology provides further insight into the dangers of self-indulgence and narcissism. Self-indulgence arises when individuals lack self-restraint, continually seeking immediate gratification. This behavior not only leads to destructive habits but also reinforces the ego's dominance. Over time, self-indulgence fosters a sense of entitlement and a diminished capacity for empathy.

Narcissism, as understood in psychology, is a pathological preoccupation with the self. Narcissistic individuals view others primarily as tools for their own validation or satisfaction. This mirrors the biblical critique of egolatry, where the self becomes an idol, overshadowing the needs of others and disrupting relationships. Narcissism often stems from deep insecurity and a desperate need for affirmation, but its effects are corrosive, leading to manipulation, exploitation, and relational breakdowns.

Jesus Christ: The Model of Self-Denial

Jesus Christ came to restore the broken relationships of humanity and creation at and large. He is the person who lives fully for others, demonstrating that true selfhood is found not in egoistic isolation but in relational love.[8] In Christ, we learn the fasting of the ego—not as punishment or self-erasure but as a spiritual discipline. Self-denial redirects us toward God's loving will, our *Summun Bonum*, and helps us resist the temptation of using others for our own satisfaction.

Self-denial, as modeled by Jesus, does not merely involve suppressing inner desires. Instead, it is about rediscovering God's desires for us and relinquishing anything that threatens our devotion to Christ: "Father, if you are willing, take this cup from me; yet not my will, but yours be done" (Luke 22:42 NIV). Jesus's life, death, and resurrection embody this practice. His journey to the cross is the ultimate act of self-denial—a rejection of the false self in favor of radical, decolonial love.

Radical love, rooted in Christ's self-denial, rejects the systems of domination, exploitation, and individualism that ego-logy naturalizes (through different leaders and institutions) across imperial and colonial stages in human history. Instead, it calls us to live in solidarity with others, especially the victims of oppressive systems, to embrace humility and to serve sacrificially. Through Jesus, we see that self-denial is not the denigration of the human self but its full liberation from the bondage of its master, selfishness.

The False Self vs. the True Self

The false self, shaped by egoism and narcissism, is an illusion that centers the self at the expense of relationality. The true self, by contrast, is discovered in Christ, who reveals that we are created to live in communion with God and others. Self-denial is the process of dismantling the barricades surrounding the false self, allowing the true self to emerge as a reflection of God's decolonial love.

This transformation is not easy. It requires us to confront the idols we have built within ourselves and to surrender our illusions of control and entitlement. Yet, in this surrender, we find freedom—the freedom to love and be loved authentically, to serve selflessly, and to live in harmony with God's purposes. Indeed, this is what enable us to fulfill the greatest commandment in Scripture: "Love the Lord your God with all your heart and with all your soul and with all your mind and with all your strength. . . . Love your neighbor as yourself. There is no commandment greater than these" (Mark 12:30, 31 NIV).

Living in Favor of Others

Through self-denial, we learn to live not for ourselves but for others. This does not mean neglecting our needs or erasing our individuality. Rather, it involves re-centering our lives around God's will and prioritizing the well-being of others. Jesus teaches us that in losing our lives for his sake, we truly find them (Matt 16:25).

In a world dominated by ego-logy and narcissistic culture, self-denial is a revolutionary act. It resists the forces of consumerism, individualism, and exploitation, inviting us into a way of life marked by mutual care, justice, and love.

SELF-DENIAL

Centering Thought

By practicing self-denial, we participate in the redemptive work of Christ, dismantling the illusions of the false self and embracing the freedom of living in God's love (*Summum Bonum*). Through this transformation, we become agents of decolonial love in a world enslaved by ego-logy and self-centeredness.

Prayer

Jesus, make me like you!
Make me a person who denies themselves to follow you.
Help me fast from my false self
and discover the true self you created me to be.
Free me from ego-logy and selfishness,
that I may live in favor of others,
embodying your decolonial love in a world of self-indulgence.

Personal Journal Prompts

- What feelings or thoughts arise when you hear the term "self-denial"? How do these reflect your current relationship with your ego?
- How do you react when asked to give up something you deeply enjoy? What does this reveal about your attachments and priorities?
- Reflect on Jesus's acts of self-denial. How can you embody his example in your daily life, especially in relationships with others?

Day 5

Renunciation
The Preferential Option for Jesus

Scripture

Don't be conformed to the patterns of this world, but be transformed by the renewing of your minds so that you can figure out what God's will is—what is good and pleasing and mature.

—Romans 12:2 CEB

Renunciation as Christian Origin

To find true happiness, we must all renounce something. From a Christian perspective, renunciation involves a voluntary decision to live in conformity to Jesus Christ in the present moment, namely, in self-denial because of Jesus Christ. We have a great cloud of witnesses bearing testimony to this way of life. In antiquity, desert Christians practiced renunciation as an expression of their death to the world (system).

People from all spheres of life threw themselves into the inhospitable deserts of Egypt and Judea. The one reason they gave to their relatives and friends for such a bizarre decision was their clear conviction of a call to "renounce the world," leaving it all behind to imitate their Lord and Savior. Later on, the Latin phrase *imitatio Christi* came to describe such a lifestyle. Men and women, young and old, rich and poor, learned and illiterate, dared to willfully submit to the ferocity of their own vices right there in the midst of the desert, where supposedly there was no other place to run to.

Cruciformity as the Preferential Option for Jesus

The various spiritual disciplines and rigor these Christians submitted to may be perceived as extremism by the contemporary observer. Disciplines such as solitude, sexual abstinence, serving the poorest of the poor, and simplicity do not align with our pursuit of the American dream and a flourishing life. Indeed, our contemporary lifestyles seem to resemble a direct opposition or can easily be found at the other end of these disciplines. Desert Christians understood being dead to the world as not being affected by the praise or contempt of others. They lived in a constant struggle to develop the virtues and character of Jesus as they received them in early Christianity. Their assignment was *imitatio Christi*, refusing to conform to the popular patterns of their time, because of Jesus and for the sake of Jesus.

Renunciation is not a theory or aspiration; it is a praxis involving both a moment of decision and a journey of perseverance in conforming to the way of Jesus Christ. The power to renounce the world (system) is born from self-denial, which can be described as the preferential option for Jesus Christ above all causes or ideals. Self-denial, as we saw in day 4, entails a serious confrontation with our ego-logy, narcissism, and revered ideologies, which inform our loyalties and vocation.

How Ancient Christopraxis Helps Correct the Errors of Modern Orthodoxy

Modern Western translations of Scripture provide two perspectives about the term "world" that might seem contradictory: (1) God loves the world (John 3); and (2) we should not love the world (1 John 2). These two meanings of "world" in the modern Bible are distinct. The first refers to creation, the product of divine work—God's world. The second refers to ideologies, thoughts, attitudes, actions, systems, and institutions that are contrary to divine *shalom* (peace) and justice. Many ancient Mediterranean Christians eventually had to renounce their beloved ideologies, guilds, and vocations because they realized God's love for the created world, hence, renouncing all ideas, attitudes, actions, and systems that destroy divine *shalom* and justice.

Augustine of Hippo is a case in point. Having adopted a Manichean philosophy, in which dualism attributed inherited evil to material existence (created world), he came to the realization of evil as *privatio boni*: "All things that exist are good, insofar as they exist; evil is the privation of good, a lack or absence of being."[9]

Many desert Christians embraced what is called Docetism and Origenism, which attributed evil to matter; however, many came to realize that God was mysteriously present amid created beings and nature and, hence, came to find God in places and bodies they thought were evil-possessed. They lived in the desert (place of demons), talked and cohabited with wild animals, healed the body and mind of many visitors, served the poor, etc. Many desert Christians were able to correct and renounce their own ideological errors because of their commitment to Christopraxis, *imitatio Christi*.

From Renunciation to Interculturality

Jesus Christ became flesh in the world, in culture, and in society as an act of divine self-revelation so that we could be reconciled with God, ourselves, and creation. This cosmic intersection is the ultimate effort of the divine in order to concretely experience historical shalom and justice. In Jesus Christ, we learn to value culture as a divine gift and discern good and evil within it, aiming to renew our own cultures as resurrected cultures—a vessel for transmitting *shalom* and justice. In Jesus Christ, we learn to live according to the culture of God's kingdom, not as a denial of our native cultures but as an amplification of them, in the Spirit, to reflect God's perichoretic interculturality. Renunciation for Jesus's sake is the effort to live in this human-created world with the values and practices of God's unfolding kingdom—being blessed, being light, being salt, being hope, and being the people of tomorrow.

Centering Thought

In the current context where political ideologies, religious nationalism, racism, sexism, Islamophobia, antisemitism, and ecological destruction are so pervasive, we urgently need to relearn a probiotic theology of renunciation informing a Christopraxis that corrects our antibiotic ideological errors.

Prayer

Jesus, make me like you!
Help me embrace my desert, to confront my
vices and cultivate my virtues.
Liberate me from my false orthodoxy through your Christopraxis.
Jesus, make me like you!
Make me a person who renounces injustice,
embraces cruciform love,
and opts for you in every moment, everywhere.

Personal Journal Prompts

- Reflect on your experiences with renunciation. What does renouncing the world (system) mean to you personally? How does this align with your faith journey?
- Consider your sociocultural background. What aspects of your culture and social class do you see as good and beneficial, and which parts do you believe contradict the values of God's unfolding kingdom?
- Identify specific areas of your life (politics, art, sports, entertainment, missions). What must you renounce that goes against God's unfolding kingdom on behalf of more justice and *shalom* in the world? How can you take practical steps to live out these values daily?

Day 6

Charity in a World of Philanthropists

Scripture

*I assure you
that when you have done it
for one of the least of these brothers and sisters of mine,
you have done it for me.*

—Matthew 25:40 CEB

Charity: The Radical Act of Love

WE ALL NEED CHARITY to be happy. Charity is more than almsgiving or superficial generosity in the form of public or private philanthropy—it is the embodiment of care, esteem, respect, and dialogue. It stands in stark opposition to indifference and apathy. Indifference renders others invisible, as if they do not exist. Apathy builds walls of distance between us, fostering loneliness and erasing the relational value of others. Others become things rather than people like us.

Indifference is not a neutral act but a form of violence against community. It denies the inherent dignity of the other and severs the bonds of mutuality that sustain human flourishing. In contrast, charity reaffirms the sacredness of every person, breaking through the isolation imposed by societal neglect and injustice.

Charity is the visible expression of an invisible worship—a concrete affirmation of our love for God through our love for others. As Christians, we are not charitable to appear virtuous or to earn moral accolades. Rather, we are charitable because we are good people formed by the love of God. Charity arises from a strong relationship with our merciful Creator and reflects the character of divine love in action.

Charity as a Challenge to Liberal and Conservative Philanthropy

In a world marked by systemic inequality and the rise of disruptive philanthropy, charity cannot be confined to personal acts of kindness or welfare policies shaped by partisan agendas. In many developed countries, such as the United States, democracy and public governance have been increasingly influenced by neoliberal entrepreneurialism. Even under liberal political leadership, public philanthropy typically associated with left-leaning policies has been overshadowed by disruptive philanthropy aligned with conservative approaches.

As Aaron Horvath and Walter Powell highlight in "Contributory or Disruptive: Do New Forms of Philanthropy Erode Democracy?," disruptive philanthropy seeks to "change the conversation" by using media influence to shape public discourse and amplify innovative solutions to social problems.[10] It emphasizes competition as a transformative force, prioritizing startups and alternative strategies while experimenting with novel funding models for public goods. While these approaches aim to fill gaps left by underfunded state policies, they often inadvertently undermine the legitimacy of government infrastructure.

This form of philanthropy gained prominence during Donald Trump's first presidential term and is likely to intensify in the wake of the 2024 elections, potentially eroding traditional democratic channels for public welfare. In such times, charity must be reclaimed as a Christian declaration of human dignity and care in the public sphere. It represents a resistance against systems of oppression that either render the vulnerable "invisible" through public policy in the case of liberalism or reduce them to mere transactions in a marketplace of philanthropic entrepreneurialism in the case of conservatism.

Charity, understood in this way, stands in opposition to the apathy of neoliberal individualism that prioritizes profit over people and economic efficiency over communal care. However, charity is not a substitute for justice but a necessary complement to it. While justice confronts structural sin, charity operates in the immediate and interpersonal realm, repairing relationships and healing the wounds inflicted by systems of exploitation. Political theologians like Gustavo Gutiérrez remind us that charity must aim toward liberation; it is not merely a temporary remedy for the wounds of oppression but a transformative practice that envisions a world where such wounds no longer occur.[11]

When we embody charity, we challenge the transactional logic that dominates our culture. In a society that commodifies human worth, charity restores the dignity of those relegated to the margins. It is a revolutionary act, grounded in the life and teachings of Jesus Christ, who affirmed the dignity of the poor, healed the sick, and embraced the rejected. Through charity, we participate in Christ's redemptive mission, offering a counternarrative to the dehumanizing forces of our time.

Charity, Empathy, and Suffering

Charity as a transformative practice aims at fostering both, individual and communal well-being. A praxis of charity, for Christian communities or any community, enhances empathy, reduces self-centeredness, and builds meaningful connections. From a psychological perspective, charity disrupts the isolating effects of modern life by fostering a sense of shared humanity and generosity.

However, charity also requires vulnerability. It calls us to step outside the comfort of apathy and risk engaging with the suffering of others. This emotional and spiritual labor reflects the sacrificial love of Christ, who bore the burdens of humanity out of divine charity. Divine charity may be understood as a circular pathway of empathy and redemption characterized by: self-emptying, descending ego, sacrificial service, profound empathy and vulnerability, and re-emergence as new creation (Phil 2:5–11).

At its core, charity is relational and from below. It invites us into a deeper understanding of ourselves, our neighbors, and God. Through charity, we confront the psychological barriers of fear, prejudice, and indifference, allowing God's love to reshape our hearts.

Jesus Christ: The Face of Divine Charity

Charity, through the lens of decolonial Christology, is an act of profound solidarity with those whom colonial and imperial systems have rendered disposable. It is not an expression of pity or paternalism but a radical identification with the oppressed, modeled after Jesus Christ.

As the embodiment of divine charity, Jesus lived in favor of the marginalized, actively disrupting the hierarchies of his time. His life, death, and resurrection reveal a love that prioritizes the weak and vulnerable, challenging systems of power that perpetuate exclusion and inequality. In Christ, charity is not a one-sided benevolent act performed by the powerful for the powerless as contemporary philanthropies; rather, it is rooted in mutuality and humility. Decolonial charity dismantles the logic of domination and affirms the shared humanity of all people, recognizing that the vulnerable bear the image of God and reveal Christ's presence in the world.

God's gift of Jesus to humanity is the ultimate act of charity—a love that gives without expectation of return, and yet it carries us back to abundant life in God. In Christ, we learn the labor of love, especially for those who cannot repay us. Charity becomes an expression of God's love when directed toward the most vulnerable: the hungry, the sick, the poor, and the oppressed. When we serve "the least of these," we serve Christ himself, for he is made flesh in the faces of those in need.

Charity is not about grand gestures; it manifests in daily acts of care and attention. It is about seeing the invisible, hearing the unheard, and valuing the devalued. Each act of charity becomes a moment of resistance against systems of oppression and a testimony to the gospel of life. In embodying Christ's charity, we participate in his redemptive mission, offering hope and restoration in a world fractured by inequality and indifference.

Centering Thought

Through charity, we become participants in God's praxis of social healing and personal restoration. Charity calls us to step beyond indifference and apathy, embodying the radical, decolonial love of Christ in every encounter with the people and systems we face. It is through this love that we honor the sacredness of every person and reveal the presence of God in the world.

Prayer

Jesus, make me like you!
Make me a person who embodies charity,
sees the invisible,
and loves without expectation of return.
Teach me to labor in love,
to care for the weak and vulnerable,
and to serve you in every face or system I encounter.

Personal Journal Prompts

- Has someone ever been charitable to you? How did it feel, and how did it impact your life?
- How can you be more charitable, particularly toward those who are weak or marginalized in society?
- Reflect on how your acts of charity could also challenge systems of injustice. How can you combine personal charity with a commitment to social transformation?

Day 7

Cleansing of Character and Spiritual Freedom

Scripture

*I am the true vine, and my Father is the gardener.
He cuts off every branch in me that bears no fruit,
while every branch that does bear fruit
he prunes so that it will be even more fruitful.*

—JOHN 15:1–2 NIV

The Need for Cleansing in a Complex World

CLEANSING OF CHARACTER IS essential for a life of joy and purpose. Just as our physical bodies require hygiene, our inner being—our emotions, thoughts, and character—needs regular care and refinement. We often live in environments saturated with toxicity: cultures of envy, selfishness, deceit, and apathy. Over time, these influences can distort our perception of what is mutually beneficial, leading us to think, *Most people are competitive, dishonest, and self-serving—that's just the way life is.*

This normalization of dysfunction distances us from God, others, and even ourselves. Cleansing of character, however, is God's gentle and transformative work, likened to the pruning of a vine. The Divine Gardener, with precision and care, removes what hinders growth, enabling us to bear the fruit of the Spirit: love, joy, peace, patience, kindness, goodness, faithfulness, humility, and self-control (Gal 5:22–23). This process is not merely an act of divine will but a collaboration between God's grace and our willingness to submit to the pruning process.

Emotional Health and Leadership

In the North American intercultural and multiethnic context, Christian discipleship is often burdened by the pressures of perfection and cultural expectations. Pete Scazzero's emotionally healthy leadership framework[12] offers helpful insights into the importance of character cleansing for leaders and disciples alike:

1. **Breaking the image of the perfect leader:** Many leaders feel pressured to present themselves as flawless, suppressing their vulnerabilities and personal needs. Cleansing of character begins with authenticity—a willingness to admit weaknesses and struggles. This honesty deepens connections with others and models a path of self-acceptance and growth.

2. **Balancing service with rest:** The demand for sacrificial service often leads leaders to neglect their own well-being. Jesus modeled rhythms of work and rest, withdrawing to be with the Father. Emotional health calls us to embrace Sabbath rest as part of our discipleship, allowing God to prune away exhaustion and burnout.

3. **Embracing vulnerability in a culture of honor and shame:** Vulnerability is often misunderstood as weakness, especially in cultures shaped by honor and shame dynamics. However, character cleansing requires us to confront and share our struggles, creating spaces for communal healing and growth. Scazzero's focus on vulnerability aligns with Henri Nouwen's

teaching that true freedom comes from embracing our fragility as a channel for God's grace.

A Christlike Character: Nouwen's Perspective

Henri Nouwen's *The Inner Voice of Love* complements the emotionally healthy discipleship model by focusing on the transformative power of vulnerability and communal healing:

1. **Moving from solitude to solidarity:** Nouwen emphasizes that spiritual health begins in solitude but must move toward solidarity. A cleansed character reflects compassion and connection with others, transforming individual healing into collective liberation. This is especially significant in multiethnic contexts where community and mutual support are central to identity and faith.

2. **Recognizing fragility as strength:** Accepting our fragility is countercultural, particularly in contexts where strength and authority are highly valued. Nouwen teaches that our wounds, when surrendered to God, become sources of healing for others.[13] This mirrors Scazzero's call for vulnerable leadership, encouraging us to see our imperfections as opportunities for grace.[14]

3. **Transforming pain into freedom:** For Nouwen, freedom is found in the unconditional love of God. Cleansing of character is not about striving for perfection but embracing God's love, which liberates us from the need for performance or approval. In a multiethnic and multilingual North American context, where diverse cultural expectations to assimilate or accept essentialism often create tension, this freedom allows disciples to rest in their fluid identities as beloved children of a multicolored God.

In the Spirit: A Cleansing for Liberation

From a decolonial theological perspective, cleansing of character may also constitute an act of resistance against systems of oppression that distort our relationships with God, others, and creation. Colonial ideologies and cultural designs often promote competition, exploitation, and individualism, shaping our character in ways that reflect domination and segregation rather than cooperation and communion.

Jesus Christ in the Spirit, as the ultimate decolonial healer and liberator,[15] offers a counternarrative. His life, death, and resurrection cleanse us of the false colonial fictions of self-sufficiency; a sense of self-power to control others through systemic operations, calling it prosperity and personal fulfillment. Jesus invites us to embrace a character shaped by humility, solidarity, and sacrificial love—a character that reflects God's justice and compassion.

In this light, cleansing of character becomes a communal and political act. It is not merely about personal growth but about becoming agents of reconciliation and restoration in a fractured world. By submitting to God's pruning, we allow ourselves to be transformed into vessels of decolonial love, embodying Christ's mission to heal and restore.

The Journey Toward Wholeness

Cleansing of character is not a one-time event but a lifelong journey of emotional and spiritual growth. It requires repentance, forgiveness, and an openness to God's ongoing work in our lives. It also calls us to nurture practices of prayer, solitude, and communal accountability, creating space for God's grace to flow through us in the public sphere.

Through this process, we are freed from the colonial fictions and distortions of self-power that keep us from fully living out our calling. As Scazzero and Nouwen remind us, healing comes not from perfection but from authenticity, vulnerability, and trust in God's love.

Centering Thought

Cleansing of character is the path to wholeness and freedom. Through God's pruning, we become agents of healing and hope, reflecting the love and justice of Christ in a world longing for a different journey of transformation.

Prayer

Jesus, make me like you!
Make me a person with a cleansed and healthy character,
free to embrace my fragility as a channel of your grace.
Help me submit to the Gardener's pruning,
to grow in love, joy, and peace,
and to reflect your justice and compassion in every aspect of my life.

Personal Journal Prompts

- Reflect on moments of pain in your life. Where do you see God's presence in those times? What did you learn or unlearn?
- What areas of your character need cleansing or pruning from colonial fictions of self-sufficiency and self-serving privilege? How can you invite the Spirit, the Decolonial Healer, into this process?
- How can you, as a leader or disciple, move from a place of perfection to a place of authenticity, vulnerability, and trust in Christ's love?

Day 8

Moderation

Scripture

By the grace given to me I say to everyone among you: Do not think of yourself more highly than you ought, but think with sober judgment, each according to the measure of faith that God has assigned.

—Romans 12:3

The Virtue of Moderation

It is impossible to experience true happiness without moderation. Excess in any area of life is harmful, deceptive, and ultimately a barrier to authentic human flourishing. Moderation, understood as the fasting of excess, is perhaps the most universally sought-after virtue in both religious and philosophical traditions.

In Christianity, moderation is striving to live free from extremes. It has often been called the mother of all virtues. From the earliest days of the Christian faith, moderation has drawn disciples of all backgrounds—young and old, rich and poor, noble and humble—seeking its wisdom in the deserts of ascetics and the ordinary rhythms of city life.

Moderation offers a vision of a balanced, ordered, simple, and dynamic life, rooted in the reality of Christ's incarnation at the margins of affluence and power. It calls us to align our lives with the example of Jesus, avoiding both the traps of excess and the emptiness of deficiency.

Practicing Moderation: The Ascetic of the Spirit

The practice of moderation can be likened to the discipline of an ascetic. The term "ascetic" comes from the Greek word *askein*, meaning "to exercise" or "to practice." An ascetic of the Spirit is one who actively trains themselves in the virtues, striving to bear the fruit of the Spirit, starting with moderation.

Unfortunately, the term "ascetic" often carries a negative connotation to our modern ears, evoking images of extremism or self-flagellation for its own sake. However, in its truest sense, asceticism is not about extreme deprivation but disciplined practice. It is about the intentional cultivation of a life in the pursuit of happiness that reflects balance, prudence, and self-control.

In this sense, moderation becomes a spiritual exercise—a way of practicing simplicity, wisdom, and humility in our thoughts, actions, and habits. It is not passive but an active engagement with life, requiring discernment and effort in the context of community.

Jesus Christ: The Model of Moderation

Jesus Christ embodies the true balance of moderation. In the Gospels, Jesus is portrayed as the measure of what is appropriate, centered, and harmonious in life, however countercultural it might have seemed in his own time. Jesus's life and practices of radical love and justice in the face of systemic oppression and religious competition shocked his audience with moderation. And, his active moderation does continue to challenge us today. In Christ, we learn to live grounded and centered, avoiding the extremes that distract and distort us and yet move forward toward establishing God's unfolding reign of abundant life in a context of abundant death.

Living a life of moderation is far more challenging than falling into extremes. Extremism, whether in indulgence or denial, often feels easier because it requires less discernment. It is easier to use terror than to work for peace, to kill the enemy than to love the enemy. Extremism and absolute violence (right or left) work faster. Moderation, by contrast, demands a thoughtful and intentional alignment of our desires, actions, and priorities with God's will and God's ways.

Jesus, as the center of our lives and practices, calls us to live free from excesses and vices. He invites us to train ourselves in moderation and related virtues such as justice, prudence, wisdom, humility, charity, self-control, etc. Through Christopraxis, we discover the beauty and freedom of a balanced life, where we are neither consumed by overindulgence and hyper-activism nor diminished by neglect and inaction.

Moderation and Emotional Health

From the perspective of emotional health, moderation serves as a safeguard against burnout, imbalance, and impulsivity. Emotionally healthy spirituality emphasizes the importance of rhythms of life that integrate work, rest, prayer, and community.[16] Moderation supports these rhythms by creating space for reflection and preventing the overcommitment and overextension that so often plague modern life.

Moderation also fosters a healthy sense of self, rooted in humility. As Paul reminds us in Rom 12:3, we are called to think of ourselves "with sober judgment." This means rejecting inflated self-perceptions or comparisons that drive us toward unhealthy striving. Instead, moderation invites us to see ourselves as God sees us—beloved and valuable, yet called to live within the boundaries of God's design.

Moderation in a Multiethnic, Intercultural Context

In the multilingual and multiethnic contexts of North America, moderation takes on additional significance. Diverse cultural traditions may carry varying attitudes toward excess and restraint. Some cultures celebrate abundance and indulgence as signs of success, while others emphasize restraint and simplicity as marks of virtue. Moderation, in this context, becomes a bridge—helping individuals and communities find balance while respecting their unique cultural identities. Moderation leads to proper intercultural translation processes, which require active listening and mutual intelligibility before committing to an action.

Through a decolonial lens, moderation can also serve as a critique of consumerism and materialism, which often perpetuate systemic inequality and sociopolitical oppression. Jesus's life of simplicity and balance challenges the excesses of depredatory capitalism and invites us to embrace practices that prioritize the vulnerable in communal flourishing over individual accumulation.

A Call to Examine and Grow

Moderation is not merely an ideal but a practice that touches every area of life: spiritual, social, physical, mental, and financial. It calls us to examine ourselves honestly, identifying areas where we are prone to excess or neglect. This self-awareness is the first step toward transformation, as we seek God's guidance and grace to live more balanced and fruitful lives.

Finding a mentor or spiritual guide can also be invaluable in this journey. A mentor helps us identify blind spots and provides encouragement and accountability as we seek to grow in moderation. Whether through prayer, reflection, or intentional practices, moderation becomes a way of aligning our lives more closely with the example of Christ.

Centering Thought

In practicing moderation, we align our lives with the wisdom and example of Jesus Christ and the cloud of witnesses of desert spirituality. Moderation is not about deprivation but about living fully, freely, and joyfully in harmony with God, others, and ourselves. Through this discipline, we experience the beauty of a balanced life—a life that reflects the grace and peace of the gospel in harmony with creation.

Prayer

Jesus, make me like you!
Make me a person of moderation,
living free from excess and vices.
Teach me to center my life in you,
to practice simplicity and balance.

Personal Journal Prompts

- Do you consider yourself a person of moderation, or are there areas of your life marked by excess? Write down two personal stories—one of excess and another of moderation.

- Evaluate your life in various areas of your life such as physical, spiritual, intellectual, intercultural, vocational, emotional, financial, and others on a scale from one to five (one being least moderate, five being most moderate). Have close friends and peers give you feedback.

- Have you considered finding a mentor to help you address areas of excess or deficiency? Who might serve as a mentor for you, and how can you begin that relationship?

Day 9

Holiness
So Human, It Can Only Be Godly

Scripture

Pursue peace with everyone, and holiness, without which no one will see the Lord.

—Hebrews 12:14

Blessed are the pure in heart, for they will see God.

—Matthew 5:8 NIV

Holiness and the Shape of Humanity

Holiness is an essential aspect of human fulfillment, as it is the clearest means to realize our humanity. It moves us from false happiness to true blessedness, from a distorted identity imposed by colonial fictions to the uncovering of the image of God (*imago Dei*) within ourselves. A holy person is someone who lives their humanity authentically, as an expression of God's love and justice for and with others. Holiness is well-living, life as sacredness and sacredness as life abundant for others. A holy life is recognizable because it makes no difference *where* humanity is practiced; whether in private or public spaces, it is practiced with the same authenticity and without pretense or exaggeration.

To live in holiness is to live so humanly *for others* that such a life can only be Godly. Holy living is living self-aware of God's presence in every aspect of life—our journey, our relationships, and our destiny. Holiness invites us to see life as an integrated whole, where the sacred is not confined to specific rituals or spaces but permeates the entirety of our existence. The world is full of holy people classified as weak, wretched, and disposable and full of haughty people considered strong, indispensable, and saints.

The first population does not even know how holy they are, while the second population take for granted they are the chosen ones. The big surprise comes, sooner or later, when these populations meet the Holy One, the Giver of Life, who unveils the colonial fictions of the exalted ones and the unrealized significance of the humiliated ones (Matt 25).

The Simplicity of Holiness

Holiness is, at its core, a continuous and personal surrender to God's presence in the context of community. It requires the daily relinquishment of our will in every circumstance, relationship, and stage of life, recognizing that God's immediate presence guides us toward the destiny God desires. This surrender does not erase our identity and inclinations but reveals it more fully. The Creator, who knows us intimately, offers us a clearer reflection of our true inner self in the becoming. What holiness is not, for sure, is perfectionism or moral superiority, which Western traditions seem obsessed with.

Jesus Christ: An Embodiment of True Holiness

When God became human in the person of Jesus Christ, holiness was made more visible in the shape of practiced humanity. Jesus came to show us what it means to be truly human and truly holy—living a life wholly surrendered to God's will at the service of creation. In Christ, we see holiness as both possible and liberative, not through rigid legalism or sensationalism but through humble submission to God because of love.

Jesus rejected the false images of holiness often promoted by lousy human efforts—images rooted in prideful legalism, idealism, or self-serving sensationalism. True holiness, as exemplified by Jesus, is not about projecting an image of righteousness to others. It is about living before God as someone (all human beings) who deserves little yet joyfully receives and enjoys everything in solidarity with the least in society.

Paul's words in Phil 2:3 echo this truth: "Do nothing out of selfish ambition or vain conceit. Rather, in humility value others above yourselves" (NIV). Holiness is marked by humility, service, and an unwavering commitment to God's will. It is a life lived in love and for the benefit of others.

Holiness and the Rediscovery of Identity

In a world obsessed with self-definition and individualism, holiness offers a countercultural path. It calls us to rediscover our identity, not through self-promotion but through surrender to God. This surrender does not diminish us; rather, it allows us to see ourselves as God sees us—beloved, purposeful, and whole. Regretfully, imperial power and colonial designs tend to steal God's identity and function like God, demanding full obedience and submission of their subjects. Holiness, in such a case, is expressed as resistance and re-existence; martyrdom, if you will.

From a psychological perspective, this surrender aligns with the practice of letting go of false narratives and striving toward authentic living. It is the integration of our inner and outer selves, where we no longer seek validation through external achievements or the approval of others but find our worth in God's love and purpose.

Holiness, then, becomes a journey of healing and transformation. It is not about erasing our humanity but actually embracing it in alignment with God's design.

Holiness in a Multiethnic, Intercultural Context

In the multicultural and multiethnic context of North America, holiness speaks to the integration of diverse identities under the plural lordship of Christ. It challenges the segregations created by culture, race, and socioeconomic status, calling all people to live in humility and communion. Holiness in this context emphasizes the communal nature of discipleship, where we pursue forgiveness, peace, and reconciliation with one another as part of our calling to holiness.

Holiness also confronts systemic injustices that dehumanize and exclude. A decolonial understanding of holiness sees it as a commitment to restoring the dignity and humanity of those marginalized by oppressive systems. Jesus's life and ministry exemplify this, as he consistently uplifted the poor, the outcast, and the broken, demonstrating that holiness is inseparable from justice and compassion.

Living Holiness Daily

Holiness is not an unattainable ideal but a daily practice of surrender and renewal. It is about recognizing God's presence in the ordinary and allowing that awareness to shape our choices, relationships, and actions.

Through Jesus Christ and in the power of the Spirit, we are invited into a life of holiness that transforms us and the world around us. As we surrender our will to God, we become participants in

God's redemptive work, living as witnesses to the love and grace that define true holiness or authentic humanity.

Centering Thought

Holiness is the path to uncovering and embracing our true humanity. It invites us to live authentically in God's presence, embracing both the sacred and the ordinary with humility and grace. In the Spirit of Christ, we see the fulfillment of holiness—a life wholly surrendered to God, lived in love for others, and marked by joy and peace in resistance to and re-existence in the cracks and fractures of imperial structures and oppressive systems.

Prayer

Jesus, make me like you!
Make me a person who walks in holiness,
embracing our sacred humanity,
living in surrender to God's presence.
in resistance to exclusion, injustice, and oppression.

Personal Journal Prompts

- What comes to mind when you think of the word "holiness"? How does it challenge or inspire you?
- How can you grow in holiness by imitating Jesus? What specific aspects of his life and character speak to your journey?
- What practices or habits can help you embrace holiness in daily life? What do you need to renounce or adopt to live more fully your own humanity as a reflection of God's holiness in the public sphere?

Day 10

Liberation
From Letters in Red to Works in Red

Scripture

But whenever anyone turns to the Lord, the veil is taken away. Now the Lord is the Spirit, and where the Spirit of the Lord is, there is freedom.

—2 Corinthians 3:16–17 NIV

Truth and Freedom

TRUTH SETS US FREE. Only those who experience freedom can truly be happy. Yet, freedom is often misunderstood, and many of us live in prisons we do not even recognize. These prisons come in many forms, both internal and external. The most immediate and harmful prisons are those within us: false identities, unrestrained passions, emotional dependencies, self-deception, inferiority complexes, personal insecurities, and negative attitudes toward the future. These internal prisons ripple outward, creating or participating in societal, political, and ideological structures that oppress, enslave, and obstruct human flourishing.

LIBERATION

True liberation is intersectional and may begin anywhere. To dismantle external systems of oppression, we must also confront the chains that bind our inner lives. Some of us call this "decolonizing the mind and the body." Spiritually, the journey toward freedom happens when realizing God's transforming work in us as we join the decolonizing Spirit in cognitive, emotional, and structural processes of mutual liberation.

Understanding the Path to Liberation

By rejecting the ego's dominance (ego-logy), we challenge the systems that maintain this distortion of the human self as the *status quo* of the fittest and become aware of the divine liberative intervention. This is followed by surrender, the voluntary submission of our will to God's will for the sake of a life otherwise (Gk. *metanoia*). In this surrender, we discover that God has called us to live fully and freely in and through Jesus Christ in reciprocity with creation.

However, freedom in Christ is not based on a modern Western political view of the productive citizen, that is, a movement of the human will toward socioeconomic independence, cognitive self-reliance, and ontological autonomy (extreme individualism). Such an idea of independence often leads back to sin and death, theological speaking.

The freedom to which we are called in Jesus Christ centers on surrendering to God in communal mutuality and flourishes at the frontier of our ability to serve creation and our neighbors. Between this center of surrender and the frontier of service, we live as holy ones, daily renewing and transforming the world. We become free citizens of God's unfolding reign of life—interdependently, intersectionally, interpolitically, interculturally, and mutually caring.

Jesus Christ, the Liberator

Jesus Christ came to release the creative potential of God within us and guide us toward the journey of abundant life, a life experienced through a covenantal relationship with the creator and creation. He came to free us from all forms of bondage, both internal and external. He lived as a free and interdependent person, offering a model of authentic submission, liberation, and flourishing.

The crucifixion of Jesus of Nazareth, carried out under Roman law and fueled by religious bigotry, was the inevitable outcome of an unjust political, economic, and religious system. His unjust trial, brutal torture, and the systemic conspiracy against him and his mission of life for the most vulnerable served as a public testament to love and justice, exposing the oppressive systems of personal and sociopolitical sin that culminated in his violent execution.

Jesus Christ is the incarnation of the divine into real humanity and personhood, fully conscious of his creatureliness as an agency for redemptive love (historic liberation). His uncompromised mission of life abundant for all of us (John 10:10), especially the victims of oppressive systems, gestated the conditions for embracing our humanity as ecological liberation; a liberation that liberates time and space and body (history) from its deathly route apart from God.

"True Red" Letters in the Bible: The Blood-Red Praxis of Jesus

Participating in the liberative project of the unfolding reign of life is, at its core, a deeply spiritual process.[17] As my mentor Dr. Ray Anderson used to say, this involves becoming more like Jesus in praxis—Christopraxis—not merely adhering to the "red letters" that highlight Jesus's words in many modern Bible translations. The "true red" is not found solely in words about Jesus but in the prophetic witness of Jesus of Nazareth through his praxis of radical love and justice.

LIBERATION

This praxis stood firmly against the unjust systems that victimized the poor, women, the "people of the land," children, the half-blood Jews, and the conscious gentiles caught in the deadly circuits of Roman law and order (*Pax Romana*). True red is vividly displayed in the Bible through the crucifixion and the redemptive bloodshed of Jesus and his followers after him. It is a blood-red praxis—a call to actively pursue the life God has intended for us: a life marked by freedom, creativity, interdependence, and mutual care.

To be liberated in Christ is to live to the maximum of our potential, not the minimum. It means breaking free from the illusions and constraints that limit us and embracing the freedom to grow, to love, and to serve. As we are conformed to the image of Christ, we become living reflections of his kingdom, embodying the hope and renewal that he offers to the world.

True-Red Liberation in our Plural Societies

In a plural, multicultural, and multiethnic society, "true-red" liberation takes on additional layers of significance. Internal prisons such as false identity and inferiority complexes often stem from systemic injustices, such as racism, colonialism, patriarchy, and socioeconomic inequality. These structures perpetuate external prisons of exclusion and oppression, reinforcing cycles of bondage. We may call this the "colonial wound."[18]

True-red liberation in Christ offers a radical counternarrative. It calls us to dismantle the ideologies and systems that divide and dehumanize, while simultaneously addressing the inner wounds caused by these structures. Decolonial theology reminds us that Jesus's liberation is not only personal but also communal. It must incarnate in both: the "visible narratives" of Western modernity and the "hidden" spaces and bodies of coloniality. True-red liberation is a border operation of abundant life and decolonial mission deeply rooted in restoring the dignity of the marginalized and breaking the chains of systemic sin encrypted symbolically and materially in daily life.

In Christ, liberation means reclaiming the image of God within each of us, rejecting the false narratives imposed by oppressive systems, and embracing our identity as beloved children of God and Mother Earth. This true-red liberation empowers us to work for justice and reconciliation, creating spaces where all people can thrive in freedom and interdependence.

Life Abundant is Possible

The goal of true-red liberation is not merely to escape bondage (spiritualization) but to live in the fullness of life that God intends in the midst of oppression and injustice, following Jesus and his Christopraxis. This fullness is marked by hospitable inclusion, intersectional maturity, creative unity, and pluriversal growth into the "measure of the full stature of Christ" (Eph 4:13). It is a life where our capacities and gifts are fully realized in service to God, others, and creation.

Living in freedom requires daily surrender to God's transformative work. It is a journey of trust and obedience, where we allow the Holy Spirit to lead us beyond the limits of our fears and insecurities. As we are liberated, we become agents of liberation for others, reflecting the light of Christ in a world longing for freedom.

Centering Thought

True-red liberation in Christ is the journey from bondage to fullness, from terror to freedom, from the center of privilege to the margins of missions at the world's end. It is the process of becoming more like Jesus in praxis not in theory, who calls us to live in the fullness of our potential and to participate in the renewal of the world. Through him, we are made new and into a liberative and healing body—citizens of an unfolding reign of life where truth sets us free and love leads us to flourish.

LIBERATION

Prayer

Jesus, make me like you!
Make me a person free from the prisons within,
committed to live to the maximum of my potential.
annointed to follow you into true-red liberative praxis,
to embrace your truth,
and to walk in the fullness of life and freedom with others.

Personal Journal Prompts

- What internal prisons—false identities, fears, insecurities—do you recognize in your life? (You may want to ask others who know you enough.) How might God be calling you to freedom?
- If you could be free from something today, what would it be? What is holding you back from experiencing that freedom? What would be your personal cost of a true-red liberative praxis?
- Are you living to the maximum of your potential in Christ or settling for the minimum? What steps can you take to embrace the fullness of life God offers?

Day 11

Divine Order

Scripture

Then the Lord reached out his hand and touched my mouth and said to me, "I have put my words in your mouth. See, today I appoint you over nations and kingdoms to uproot and tear down, to destroy and overthrow, to build and to plant."

—Jeremiah 1:9–10 NIV

Order as a Movement Away from Oppression

DIVINE ORDER IS NOT a rigid, totalitarian solution to chaos. It is a dynamic and relational process of moving away from deception, disorientation, and fragmentation, which distort human life and mutual care. Many contemporary systems—whether religious, political, familial, or cultural—misuse the concept of order as a means of control and domination. These interpretations often perpetuate violent structures that stifle creativity, limit diversity, and enforce oppressive conformity.

Divine order, in contrast, moves us away from these distortions. It liberates us from the false narratives that sever our connections to one another and to God. It dismantles disorientation and deception, replacing them with a deeper awareness of the interconnectedness of all life. In divine order, we resist the decomposition of relationships and the distancing from mutuality, cultivating instead a life that mirrors God's justice and compassion.

Divine Order as a Rerouting Toward Abundance

In Acts 16, we see how the Holy Spirit reroutes the apostle Paul and his team, closing some doors and opening others to guide them toward the *missio Dei*, God's mission of abundant life for all. Divine order is not a linear path but a responsive, Spirit-led journey that prioritizes flourishing. This process is not about imposing rigid structures but about aligning ourselves with the rhythms of God's creative and redemptive work.

Divine order invites us to live in dynamic alignment with God's purposes. It is about embracing a posture of openness, allowing the Spirit to reroute our plans and priorities toward life-giving practices and relationships. Experienced initially as a disruption, it is a movement toward abundance—not material accumulation but the richness of mutual care, creativity, and interdependence that reflect the life of the Trinity.

Divine Order as a Declassification of Terminal Knowledge

Western modernity has often used the concept of order to classify knowledge in ways that open possibilities and developmental channels for some at the flip side of oppressive socioeconomic systems and excluding categories for others. Some African Indigenous communities call this "terminal knowledge" or "killing knowledge."

Colonial systems of thought have enforced hierarchies of knowledge, privileging certain ways of knowing while marginalizing others, particularly Indigenous, women, and non-Western populations with their own systems of knowledge. Divine order disrupts these hierarchies, offering a decolonial perspective that values all forms of wisdom as gifts from God in an ecology where all people fit.

To live in divine order is to participate in the declassification of oppressive knowledge systems. It calls us to question and dismantle the narratives that uphold domination and exploitation. Instead, divine order reorients us toward knowledge that heals, restores, and liberates. It challenges us to embrace interculturality, where diverse ways of knowing and being are honored and woven together in mutual respect and care.

Divine Order as a Healing Space

Divine order creates a space for healing, hospitality, and reintegration. It is not about eliminating chaos but transforming it into a space where life can flourish (Gen 1). In divine order, there is room for self-assurance, safety, and refuge—a sanctuary where fragmented lives and communities are made whole.

This healing space reflects God's deep care for creation. It invites us to practice hospitality, offering refuge to the vulnerable and marginalized. It encourages us to cultivate inner assurance, finding safety not in rigid control but in the presence of God's love. Divine order integrates our inner and outer lives, helping us live authentically and harmoniously with others. This demands a greater ethics and responsibility from individuals and communities than that of a homogeneous segregated society—belonging! Or, to say it with Howard Thurman, contact with communion![19]

Divine Order in Practice

1. **Religious morality:** Divine order challenges moral systems that use terror or control to enforce behavior. Instead, it cultivates a morality rooted in love, humility, and the pursuit of justice.
2. **Political structures:** Divine order resists authoritarianism and systems of oppression (right or left), advocating for political practices that prioritize the dignity and well-being of all. It calls for policies that reflect mutual care and communal flourishing.
3. **Family systems:** In families, divine order nurtures relationships of mutual respect and love. It resists hierarchical domination (Christian or non-Christian), instead promoting shared responsibilities and intergenerational support.
4. **Interculturality:** Divine order embraces cultural diversity as a reflection of God's creativity (Acts 2). It encourages dialogue and collaboration, breaking down barriers of prejudice and exclusion.
5. **Personal growth and vocations:** On a personal level, divine order provides direction and purpose. It helps us align our careers, relationships, and daily practices with God's vision for our lives, fostering a life of balance, creativity, and service.

Centering Thought

Divine order is not a static solution but a dynamic, Spirit-led process. It invites us to live in alignment with God's purposes, moving away from oppression and disconnection and toward a life of mutual care, creativity, and abundant flourishing. In practicing divine order, we become participants in the *missio Dei*, embodying the healing and hope of God's unfolding kingdom in the world.

Prayer

Jesus, make me like you!
Make me a person who lives in divine order,
moving away from deception and division,
embracing the rerouting of the Spirit,
and creating spaces of healing and hospitality.
Teach me to align my life with your purposes,
to seek knowledge that restores,
and to reflect your love in all I do.

Personal Journal Prompts

- Reflect on areas of your life where disorientation or deception has taken root. How might God be calling you to move toward divine order?
- Where have you experienced the Spirit rerouting your plans or priorities? How can you embrace this dynamic process more fully?
- In what ways can you create spaces of healing and hospitality in your relationships, community, or vocation?

Day 12

Vision and Vocation

Scripture

*You desire truth in the inward being;
therefore teach me wisdom in my secret heart.*

PSALM 51:6

*For the Lord gives wisdom;
from his mouth come knowledge and understanding.*

PROVERBS 2:6

The Necessity of Vision

WE ALL NEED VISION to live meaningfully and to be both happy and useful. Without vision, destruction ensues (Hos 4:6). In the unfolding reign of God, blindness and ignorance are synonymous. Everyone perceives life through a particular lens—frameworks shaped by culture, personal experiences, acquired mentalities, dominant relationships, and personal passions.

If God is absent from these frames of reference, we dwell in deep darkness, stumbling through life as if blind. Without divine vision, we remain ignorant, acting as enemies of God and destroyers of God's creation. Worse yet, we risk becoming "blind guides of the blind" (Matt 5:14) leading others into a culture of ignorance and darkness.

Transformative Visions

All transformative and just visions come from God. God is the source and initiator of these visions. As human beings, we are like mirrors, tasked with receiving divine visions and faithfully transmitting them to the communities for whom they are intended.

To become effective visionaries, we must deepen our intimacy with God. The early Christians referred to this effort as *ascensus mentis ad Deum*—ascending to the mind of God. This ascent requires a descent into humility, the surrender of ego, and a commitment to continuous prayer. Intimacy with God is the chamber of divine revelation.

It is within this sacred intimacy that God, by God's grace, reveals the unimaginable—new images, ideas, emotions, and scenes never before experienced. This revelation fills us with awe, leading to reverent silence. In that space, we begin to think the new, envision the inconceivable, and believe in the impossible.

Jesus Christ Came to Heal Our Vision

Jesus Christ came to heal our vision, enabling the blind to see (Luke 4). As Savior and Lord, he is both the beginning and the culmination of our healing from spiritual blindness. In Christ, we learn to see God in every human being, to value creation as sacred, and to discern what comes from God, the Enemy, and humanity.

To have vision means to be a seer of the unfolding reign of God for the sake of others. Like the prophets of old, being a seer involves seeing with God's eyes, speaking with God's words, and acting to fulfill God's will. It is a vocation that demands courage, humility, and a willingness to be transformed by what we perceive.

Regretfully, many of us begin humbly and obediently but later on end up appropriating God's vision to the point of confusing it with ours. When that happens, God stands against our own vision, because it is no longer God's but ours or the empire's. We have stolen it. It happened in biblical times and it is happening in ours. We need some checkpoints to make sure we are doing mission with God, *not against God or without God.*

Vision as a Spiritual Discipline for Doing Mission with God

1. **Intimacy with God as the source of vision:** Vision flows from a deep relationship with God. Without this intimacy, our perceptions remain clouded by ego and worldly distractions. The discipline of prayer, silence, and reflection in the context of a discerning community opens the space for divine revelation to take root in our hearts.

2. **The humility to descend in order to ascend:** Ascending to God's vision requires humility. It is a surrender of self-centeredness, an acknowledgment that true wisdom and knowledge are gifts from God, not products of our own making.

3. **Seeing through God's eyes:** Divine vision transforms how we see the world. It enables us to discern God's image in others, value the sacredness of creation, and distinguish truth from deception. This vision is not limited to spiritual insight but extends to practical action—building just communities, nurturing relationships, and stewarding creation faithfully.

4. **Visionaries for the reign of God, not for empire:** Those entrusted with divine vision bear the responsibility of transmitting it faithfully. Like the prophets, they are called to speak truth and act justly, not for personal gain but to align communities with God's will. This, inevitably, generates hostilities with imperial structures that have appropriated God to rule the land and build privilege and profit.

Vision and Mission in a Plural Society

In the diverse, multiethnic societies of today, vision must embrace intercultural translation. Cultural frameworks often shape how individuals perceive God, the world, and themselves. Without careful discernment, these frameworks can become barriers to understanding and mutual care.

Divine vision, however, transcends cultural limitations. It calls us to honor the diversity of God's creation while seeking unity in his purpose. Visionary leadership in this context involves bridging cultural divides, challenging biases, and fostering collaboration rooted in mutual respect and shared values.

The Vocation of Visionaries

To live as a visionary is to see the world as God sees it—not only as it is but as it could be. It means aligning our thoughts, words, and actions with God's redemptive purposes in the context of discerning communities. This is not a passive task; it requires intentionality, courage, and a willingness to be shaped by the visions God reveals.

Vision is not merely about seeing what others cannot; it is about acting faithfully to bring God's unfolding reign to fruition in the here and now and among ourselves. It is about speaking truth, building community, and pursuing justice with unwavering commitment. It is very costly!

Centering Thought

Divine vision is both a gift and a responsibility. It calls us to see beyond the present, to imagine the unimaginable, and to act faithfully in alignment with God's purposes. In Christ's Spirit, we are given the eyes to see, the wisdom to discern, and the courage to act, becoming visionaries of hope and healing for a world in need. In essence, this is what *ekklesia*, the church's vocation is all about.

Prayer

Jesus, make me like you!
Make me a person of vision and action,
open to the revelations of your Spirit.
Help me to descend in humility
so that I may ascend to the heights of your wisdom.
Teach me to see with your eyes,
to speak with your words,
and to act with your love,
Following your great cloud of witnesses.

Personal Journal Prompts

- Where do you currently stand in your level of intimacy with God—low, medium, or high? Who is your discerning community, and how can they support you in growing closer to God?
- Have you ever assessed your vocation in terms of doing vision and mission with God, against God, or without God? Where would you place yourself in your current stage of life?
- What vision does God desire to accomplish through you and where? Take time to reflect and invite your discerning community into this process. Write down what emerges.

Day 13

Social Responsibility
Becoming A Public Witness

Scripture

Rulers of the people and elders, if we are questioned today because of a good deed done to someone who was sick and are asked how this man has been healed, let it be known to all of you, and to all the people of Israel, that this man is standing before you in good health by the name of Jesus Christ of Nazareth, whom you crucified, whom God raised from the dead. . . . But Peter and John answered them, "Whether it is right in God's sight to listen to you rather than to God, you must judge; for we cannot keep from speaking about what we have seen and heard."

—Acts 4:8–10, 19–20

Social Responsibility and Public Theology

Social responsibility is not an optional add-on to Christian faith but an integral expression of it. To shirk this responsibility by thinking, *This is not my concern; someone else will handle it,* is to reject our calling as participants in God's work of justice and restoration. This negligence often stems from a privatized theology—one that secludes faith within the boundaries of personal piety or dogmatic tradition, disconnected from the public and collective struggles of humanity.

When Christian ministry and mission is confined to institutional preservation or abstract doctrine, it risks becoming complicit in systems of oppression. Instead of challenging the injustices of the world, it supports the *status quo*, perpetuating what Boaventura de Sousa Santos calls "abyssal thinking"—a mindset that invisibilizes the oppressed and denies their dignity and agency.[20]

Since the Christian religion has become a private occupation in modern societies, we must now embrace a public theology and witness to Jesus. A biblically energized public theology forces us to actively engage with the world's suffering. It helps us discern and make visible the redemptive action of Jesus Christ in concrete, historical contexts. Public theology calls us to move beyond privatized and dogmatic expressions of faith to a praxis-oriented, life-affirming theology rooted in the struggles for human dignity and collective liberation.

The Politics of Jesus and the Call to Public Witness

The politics of Jesus are the politics of God's unfolding kingdom— a vision of mercy, justice, joy, peace, and communal flourishing. Jesus did not isolate himself from societal structures but engaged them directly, challenging their injustices and inviting transformation. His ministry was a public, embodied testimony of God's reign, calling for the liberation of the oppressed and the restoration of broken relationships.

As followers of Jesus Christ, we are called to emulate this public witness. This involves addressing systemic injustices, advocating for the vulnerable, and embodying alternative ways of being that reflect the kingdom of God. It requires us to act with prophetic courage, speaking truth to power and modeling a culture of solidarity, hospitality, and mutual care.

Public theology transforms our understanding of what it means to be a "good Christian" or "good citizen." It reveals that our faith cannot be relegated to personal morality or institutional loyalty but must actively engage with the social, political, and cultural realities of our world.

Another Training Is Possible: From Private Faith to Public Witness

In the process of modernization, continents around the world have been reconfigured into "nation-states," where the separation of church and state is often a foundational principle. While this principle is intended to promote freedom of religion and the pursuit of democracy, in practice it has often relegated the "church" to a private endeavor, leaving it struggling to find a relevant role in the public sphere.

On one hand, the state has assumed the role of moral arbiter, while the private sector has stepped in as a disruptive philanthropist. In profit-driven states, the church tends to adopt individualistic tendencies, become a political instrument, or compete as a "soul predator," often failing to engage meaningfully in the public sphere where it could effectively perform its prophetic and priestly roles in service to the common welfare.

Regretfully, many contemporary ministers and lay leaders are not adequately prepared for this challenge. Even those who undergo formal academic training are often not equipped with the frameworks necessary to become political agents of the kingdom of God. Theological training has shifted from its origins in communal struggles for dignity and alternative living to a detached, elitist, and insular leadership formation enterprise. This privatized theological framework frequently serves the interests of its institutional promoters (denominations, networks, soul industry) rather than addressing the generational needs, the growing anxiety of urban families, and the overflowing production of oppressed and marginalized populations. It becomes a theology of *absence*—to use Boaventura de Sousa Santos's term from his sociology of absences[21]—characterized by:

- **Invisibility of the oppressed:** Privatized theology fails to acknowledge the lived realities of marginalized communities, rendering them invisible in its discourse.

- **Absence of rights and agency:** It neglects the rights and voices of those most impacted by systemic injustice, offering no meaningful pathway to liberation.

- **Complicity in oppression:** By remaining silent or disengaged, it becomes complicit in the very structures of power that perpetuate suffering.

Biblically energized public theology seeks to dismantle this privatization. At its core, a biblically energized public theology is a theology of *emergence*—reclaiming theology as a communal and life-affirming endeavor, deeply rooted in the struggles for justice, equity, and peace. It resists being confined to intellectual elites and instead arises from and serves the lived experiences of all people, particularly those at the margins.

Through a biblically energized public theology, the church can reassert its relevance in the public sphere, championing the prophetic call for justice and embodying the priestly role of healing and re-existence. By engaging directly with societal issues, public theology bridges the gap between faith and action, restoring theology to its rightful place as a transformative force for good living.

A Theology of Life and Liberation

Following Santos's sociology of emergence, to practice a biblically energized public theology is to engage in a "deprivatized" theology—a theology of life in the post-abyssal horizon.[22] This is a theology that:

1. **Reveals the truth of oppression:** It unmasks the systems and ideologies that oppress and exploit, exposing their incompatibility with the gospel.

2. **Centers the marginalized:** It listens to and amplifies the voices of those excluded by dominant structures, recognizing their agency in their own liberation.
3. **Engages in concrete action:** It combines reflection with action, embodying God's justice and mercy in practical ways.
4. **Builds communal solidarity:** It fosters alliances across cultural, social, and political boundaries, bringing together diverse communities in the shared struggle for dignity and life.

Christopraxis as Public Witness

It does not take much to see that Jesus Christ is the ultimate model of public theology. His life, death, and resurrection testify to a new social and cultural order—one rooted in mercy, justice, and solidarity. Jesus challenges us to live, not in isolation but in active engagement with the world, healing the rich and powerful, including women and children, advocating for the oppressed and holding systems of power accountable.

In Christ, we learn to embody a culture of life within the cultures of death that dominate our world. We are called to advocate for all people, beginning with the exploited; we are called to empower the vulnerable; and we are called to model God's unfolding kingdom in the public square. This is not merely an individual task but a collective calling, where the church acts as a visible sign of God's reign—a community of hope and healing in a fractured world.

Centering Thought

Social responsibility, understood as a public testimony of faith, calls us to embody the gospel in all areas of life. It challenges us to move beyond individualism and institutionalism, embracing a theology that transforms lives, communities, and systems. In Christ, we are empowered to live as agents of God's kingdom, bearing witness to the liberating power of his love and justice.

SOCIAL RESPONSIBILITY

Prayer

Jesus, make me like you!
Make me a public witness of your kingdom,
engaged in the struggles of this world
and committed to the flourishing of all people.
Help me to move beyond privatized faith
to a theology of healing and hope,
rooted in justice, mercy, and solidarity.

Personal Journal Prompts

- How have you exercised your political and social responsibility thus far? Are there areas where you have avoided engagement?
- Reflect on whether your faith has been more private or public. How can you integrate your beliefs with actions that serve the common good?
- What specific steps can you take to contribute to a culture of healing and hope in your community, workplace, or nation?

Day 14

The Social Bubble

Scripture

Abide in me, and I in you. As the branch cannot bear fruit by itself, unless it abides in the vine, neither can you, unless you abide in me. I am the vine; you are the branches . . . for apart from me you can do nothing. . . . This is my commandment, that you love one another as I have loved you.

—John 15:4, 5, 12, ESV

Individualism and the Social Bubble

Excess in any form is harmful, and this includes the excesses of individualism. Individualism, often celebrated as the cult of the self, elevates personal independence and uniqueness as the ultimate measure of value. While it is natural and important to affirm what makes us unique, when this desire becomes the rule of life, it isolates us from others, emphasizing *my perspective, my privacy, my possessions, my decisions.*

This exaggerated focus on the self can trap us in a social bubble, prioritizing individual preferences over communal relationships and creating an "against-those-like-us" mentality. It disconnects us from the mutual interdependence essential for human flourishing, making the myth of the detached individual not only harmful but dangerous to societal well-being.

The Myth of Independence

The idea of a completely self-sufficient individual is a fallacy. Human beings are inherently relational, shaped by our bonds with others and the traditions that nurture us. Community functions as the womb of our individual and social identity. It is through our relationships that we grow, learn, and discover who we are.

While individuality is essential for personal identity, taking responsibility and exercising agency, it must be understood as part of a larger whole. The "I" exists in the context of the "us." What is mine is defined in relation to what is yours, and vice versa. Our individual identity is not isolated but emerges through mutual dependence and shared growth. To bear God's image is to live in this web of relationships—with God, with others, and with creation. This interconnectedness is not optional or situational; it is a fundamental reality of human existence.

Jesus Christ: The Bond of Community

Jesus Christ is the ultimate fulfillment of existence as one bound to God, humanity, and creation. He mediates the bond between Creator and creation, between one person and another and the cosmos. Through Jesus, we are connected to God and learn what it means to live bound to one another in cosmic love and justice.

In Christ, our individuality is neither erased nor idolized but integrated into the community of faith. He teaches us to see ourselves not as individuals merely *in* the community but as individuals *of* the community—connected, interdependent, and mutually responsible.

Jesus modeled this life through his actions: serving his disciples, advocating for the marginalized, and cultivating bonds of trust and mutual care. In him, we learn to reject the isolating tendencies of the social bubble and embrace a life of relational accountability and shared purpose. In fact, we are commanded to do just that: "This is my commandment, that you love one another as I have loved you" (John 15:12).

Community as a Sacred Space

Community is not just a practical arrangement; it is a sacred space where we encounter God and realize our true humanity. In a world increasingly shaped by isolation, competition, and transactional relationships, true community stands as a countercultural testimony to the kingdom of God.

Living in community means embracing the vulnerabilities and strengths of others, recognizing that our well-being is tied to theirs. It involves practicing humility, forgiveness, and generosity, knowing that these virtues bind us together and reflect God's presence among us.

Social Bubbles in Diverse Contexts

In plural societies, social bubbles often take the form of tribalism, where individuals and groups retreat into cultural, political, or ideological silos. This retreat creates barriers that hinder meaningful interaction and foster hostility toward difference. Tribalism amplifies an "us-versus-them" mentality, eroding the potential for pluralistic societies to thrive on mutual respect and shared purpose. These social bubbles perpetuate exclusion, reinforcing biases and isolating communities from the broader relational networks that sustain human flourishing.

A dear friend and colleague, the psychologist Pamela King, along with Jack Balswick and Kevin Reimer, have articulated a helpful concept called "the reciprocating self," which offers an alternative vision.[23] They emphasize that individuals develop their fullest sense of identity, not in isolation but through relationships characterized by mutuality and interdependence. A reciprocating self understands that personal growth is tied to the growth and well-being of others. This perspective challenges the tribalistic tendencies of social bubbles, calling individuals and groups to transcend self-interest and engage in reciprocal relationships that nurture collective flourishing.

Similarly, Boaventura de Sousa Santos's concept of "intercultural translation" provides a critical framework for breaking down the walls of tribalism.[24] Intercultural translation encourages dialogue across cultural and ideological boundaries, seeking common ground while respecting difference. It is a practice of mutual learning that values diverse perspectives without erasing their uniqueness. In the context of social bubbles, intercultural translation becomes a vital tool for fostering understanding, building trust, and creating inclusive spaces where non-relativist pluralism can thrive.

Living in Christ calls us to move beyond tribalism and the isolation of social bubbles. It demands that we embrace a life of intercultural engagement, rooted in the recognition of our interconnectedness as bearers of God's image.

Living Beyond the Social Bubble

To live beyond the social bubble is to reject tribalism and embrace the relational dynamism of "the reciprocating self." It is to recognize that our individual identities are inextricably tied to the communities and networks we inhabit. This relational identity is not a loss of self but a fuller realization of it through mutuality, interdependence, and shared purpose.

In a plural society, this requires intentional efforts to counteract the divisive forces of tribalism.

By engaging in "intercultural translation," we learn to navigate cultural and ideological differences with humility and curiosity. This practice allows us to see the value in others' experiences and perspectives, fostering relationships that are both reciprocal and transformative.

In Christ, we are given the ultimate example of living beyond the social bubble. Jesus modeled a life of radical inclusivity and relational reciprocity, breaking down cultural, social, and religious barriers to create a new kind of community. His ministry was not confined to any one group or ideology but extended to all, inviting everyone into a shared vision of God's unfolding kingdom. Jesus's dining table, in other words, was big enough for everyone, including his enemies. How about ours?

To follow Jesus's example is to live as a reciprocating self, deeply connected to God and others, and committed to the work of intercultural translation. It means rejecting the false safety of tribalism and social bubbles, choosing instead to engage with the complexities and richness of a pluralistic world with radical hospitality in decolonial love. This life of relational engagement not only reflects the character of Christ but also contributes to the healing and renewal of our fractured societies.

Centering Thought

Let us transcend our social bubbles by embracing the relational essence of our humanity as illustrated by Jesus. This balances individuality with interdependence, fostering intercultural dialogue that values diversity while seeking shared purpose. By rejecting isolation and engaging in mutual responsibility, we embody the transformative power of Christ's reconstituting love, becoming active participants in the healing and renewal of our communities and the world

Prayer

Jesus, make me like you!
Make me an individual bound to God and others.
Teach me to see beyond myself, my reciprocating self,
to embrace community in diversity with humility and grace.
Help me to become an intercultural translator,
serving others as a witness to your kingdom.

Personal Journal Prompts

- Do you know yourself well enough to identify what makes you unique? How does your individuality contribute to the community around you? How does being in proximity to a diverse community challenge you?
- How important is living in connection with others to you? Are there areas where you prioritize independence at the expense of community?
- How did Jesus strengthen the bonds of his community? What specific practices can you adopt to follow his example in your own relationships?

Day 15

Secrets

Scripture

*For everything there is a season,
and a time for every matter under heaven . . .
a time to keep silence, and a time to speak.*

—Ecclesiastes 3:1, 7

The Nature of Secrets

WE ALL HOLD SECRETS. At times, we resist being fully known, as though we were specimens under a microscope. We have all likely said, *No one really knows how I feel; no one fully understands me.* Secrets carry both power and vulnerability.

Some secrets bring happiness and security; others rob us of joy. When we hide lies out of fear, we live in perpetual unease. These kinds of secrets make us vulnerable, for eventually they come to light, often with destructive consequences. In such cases, we may spend our lives constructing layers of deception to protect ourselves or others, yet this only deepens our captivity. Liberation requires us to "die" to fear and "rise" to freedom through the truth.

Other secrets, however, can be life-giving. When we exercise discretion by temporarily withholding a truth for a constructive purpose, these secrets make us wise and influential. Their aim is not concealment but preservation until the appropriate moment. They protect, nurture, and empower others, enabling us to build relationships rooted in trust and care.

Secrets in Divine Perspective

Across world religious traditions and philosophies, secrets are recognized as profound elements of human existence. The Buddha emphasized the importance of truth-telling as a path to enlightenment, warning against deceit as a root of suffering. Similarly, Confucian teachings uphold *zhong* (loyalty) and *xin* (trustworthiness), reminding us that discretion, when rooted in moral purpose, sustains harmonious relationships.

Philosophers such as Søren Kierkegaard reflect on secrets as part of the human journey toward authenticity.[25] Kierkegaard suggests that transparency before God is essential to true selfhood, for only in divine communion can our inner life find coherence. This aligns with the biblical principle that while humans see outward appearances, God sees the heart (1 Sam 16:7).

In Christian theology, Jesus Christ may be described as the great secret of God, revealed in the fullness of time (*kairos*). For centuries, this divine mystery was hidden, awaiting the moment when God's love and justice would be unveiled through the incarnation. Jesus embodies the ultimate paradox: God visible in human form, forgiving the wicked, loving enemies, and offering salvation to those who least deserve it.

Jesus Christ teaches us the wisdom of discretion and the liberation of truth. He exposes the destructive power of deceit and fear while demonstrating the redemptive power of prudent secrecy. He knows the deepest secrets of God and the human heart, weighing them with truth and grace. In him, we find both the cornerstone that supports prudent secrecy and the stumbling block that confronts deceitful secrecy.

Living with Secrets: A Balance of Prudence and Freedom

Secrets are inevitable, but their impact depends on their nature and intent. The challenge lies in discerning whether a secret binds us in fear or empowers us with wisdom. The wisdom traditions across the world suggest that secrets should not be used to manipulate or oppress but to protect and nurture.

Prudent secrecy serves a purpose. It is the ability to safeguard truth until the right moment, much like a farmer waiting for the proper season to harvest. This approach reflects divine wisdom, recognizing that timing matters in revealing truths. However, living under the shadow of fearful secrets diminishes our humanity, keeping us captive to lies and coercion. True liberation comes when we confront such secrets in the light of truth.

In a world filled with secrecy—political, social, and personal—our task as individuals and communities is to discern how to handle the secrets we carry. Are they tools for healing or weapons of harm? Are they seeds of growth or roots of deception?

Secrets in Intercultural and Public Contexts

In a diverse and interconnected world, secrecy often plays a role in power dynamics. Cultural taboos and systemic inequalities can render certain truths invisible, perpetuating oppression. Decolonial thinkers emphasize the need to unveil hidden truths that colonial and hegemonic systems suppress, particularly regarding marginalized peoples and histories.

Yet, secrecy can also serve a protective function. In many Indigenous traditions, sacred knowledge is safeguarded to preserve its integrity and protect communities from exploitation. This highlights the importance of respecting the boundaries of cultural secrets while challenging harmful silences that perpetuate injustice.

Living as responsible stewards of secrets requires us to balance these dimensions—discerning when to speak and when to remain silent, always guided by the principles of justice, love, and mutual care.

Centering Thought

Secrets are part of the human experience, but they must be handled with wisdom and care. In Christ, we find both the courage to confront destructive secrecy and the prudence to preserve life-giving truths. Through this balance, we learn to live authentically, reflecting the justice and love of God in every aspect of our lives.

Prayer

Jesus, make me like you!
Make me a person liberated from lies and terror,
yet wise enough to guard what must be kept.
Teach me the balance of truth and discretion,
to live in freedom and build others up
through the power of love and prudence.

Personal Journal Prompts

- What secrets do you currently hold? Are they life-giving or destructive?
- Have you considered the potential harm or benefit of revealing or keeping these secrets?
- What might Jesus be calling you to do with your secrets? How can they align with truth, freedom, and love? How do your secrets build or bound vulnerable people?

Day 16

Aspirations

Scripture

For it is God who works in you to will and to act in order to fulfill his good purpose.

—Philippians 2:13 NIV

The Power of Aspirations

Aspirations reflect a desire to live, grow, and find happiness. In contrast, the absence of aspirations signals complacency—a form of worshiping the *status quo*. Aspirations arise from personal vision and a sense of self-worth, whereas complacency is a mindset that settles for the norms of the majority, often leading to minimal effort and unrealized potential.

Complacency is frequently mistaken for contentment, but the two are fundamentally different. Complacency adopts the existing standard without striving to surpass it. Contentment, however, is a spiritual discipline that teaches us to give thanks to God in all circumstances, appreciating what we have while remaining open to growth. Ironically, many who are complacent lack true contentment.

Aspirations That Build

Well-grounded aspirations energize us, filling our lives with dreams and achievements. Misguided aspirations—rooted in greed, vanity, or a lust for power—lead to personal and societal harm. Yet, aspirations that are rightly oriented inspire personal and communal development, motivating us to cultivate our innate talents and acquired skills for the greater good.

Healthy aspirations are not merely self-serving; they contribute to a larger purpose. They challenge us to expand our horizons, nurture creativity, and invest in the well-being of others. Aspirations become a pathway to flourishing when they align with our unique gifts and the collective needs of our communities.

Aspirations in Christ

Jesus Christ fulfills the highest aspirations of humanity: knowing God intimately, overcoming death, living with constructive purpose, becoming agents of change, and using our gifts to build others up. In Christ, we learn to desire more of God, to expect more from others, and to give more of ourselves for causes greater than our own—the work of God's unfolding kingdom.

Aspirations in Christ are transformative. They free us from the narrow ambitions of self-promotion and align us with God's redemptive purposes. In him, we discover a vision for our lives that is both personal and communal, marked by hope, generosity, and service.

Aspirations in a Broader Context

World religions and philosophies affirm the importance of aspirations. In Buddhism, the concept of "right effort" encourages individuals to cultivate aspirations that lead to enlightenment, rooted in wisdom and compassion. In Indigenous traditions, aspirations often center on harmony with the land and communal well-being, reflecting a holistic vision of life. Philosophers from Aristotle to modern thinkers emphasize that aspirations guide us toward *eudaimonia*—a flourishing life grounded in virtue and purpose.

Incorporating these perspectives, aspirations take on a dual role: personal development and collective responsibility. They become a bridge between individual growth and societal transformation, aligning our personal goals with the greater good.

Living with Aspirations

To live with aspirations is to reject complacency while practicing contentment in the power of the Spirit. It is to recognize that our potential is not just for ourselves but for the flourishing of others. Aspirations rooted in God's will and informed by our unique talents create a framework for meaningful living.

This requires self-reflection and discernment. Are our aspirations driven by selfish ambition, or do they align with God's purposes? Are they rooted in love for others and the desire to serve, or do they reflect fleeting desires for personal gain?

In Christ through the Spirit, we find the ultimate model of aspirational living. Jesus's life demonstrates a balance of contentment and vision—grounded in faith, motivated by love, and directed toward the renewal of all things.

Centering Thought

Aspirations are a gift from the Spirit, a reflection of our desire to grow, serve, and live meaningfully. In Christ, our aspirations are elevated beyond self-interest, becoming pathways to transformation—for ourselves, our communities, and the world. Through Christ's Spirit, we are empowered to pursue dreams that honor God and bring life to others.

ASPIRATIONS

Prayer

Jesus, make me like you!
Make me a person with aspirations
aligned with your will and kingdom.
Teach me to dream with purpose,
to nurture my gifts in the Spirit,
and to give myself fully to causes
greater than my own.

Personal Journal Prompts

- What aspirations from your past have faded and why?
- What aspirations have been fulfilled in your life, and how have they shaped you?
- Are your current aspirations rooted in God's will and your unique talents? How can you refine them to serve both personal growth and the common good?

Day 17

Conviviality
A Probiotic Theology

Scripture

For where two or three are gathered in my name, I am there among them.

—Matthew 18:20

Desiring Life Together in a World of Life Apart

WE ARE RELATIONAL CREATURES of dialogue, born to communicate and share life together. These interpersonal and intercultural competencies have made us survive as a species and brought us happiness, giving life a sense of joy and meaning. In contrast, there is a *contra natura* proclivity to living in segregation that leads to falling into the excess of individualism and subjecting us to social diseases such as apathy, marginalization, racism, or discrimination. We may call this proclivity an expression of our sinful nature.

When we fall into these social vices, it becomes difficult to believe that dialogue and life together can energize, affirm, and propel us to the fullness of life, the celebration of difference, and the joy of conviviality. Reading the first chapters of the book of Genesis illustrates this without question (3:10–12; 4:6–13; 11).

Thinking, *There are no other people with whom we can share our joys and sorrows because ultimately everyone is self-interested and trying to take advantage of us*, reflects a deep mistrust in humanity and a spirit of social dysfunction. Such thoughts may signal psychological disorders such as paranoia, social anxiety, post-traumatic stress, depression, borderline personality, and even schizophrenia. If we think this way, we are renouncing all possibilities of redemption and human life together as a good creation of God; we have condemned ourselves and neutralized the work of Jesus on the cross for us and others.

God has more faith in humanity than we do in ourselves (John 3:16). God sees beyond our wicked actions; God sees us through the lens of new creation in his Son Jesus Christ (Eph 2:10). God believes in us and knows we are capable of living in favor of our neighbor and not against them. The Creator has not finished working in us just yet. Can you believe this?

Global Mistrust and Monocultural Dysfunctionality

Mistrust in humanity often stems from negative personal experiences, creating barriers that prevent us from engaging in meaningful relationships. Overcoming this mistrust requires us to embrace in concrete ways the teachings of Jesus (Christopraxis), who calls us to love our neighbors and live in community. Reflect on your personal experiences and identify ways to rebuild trust and open yourself to others.

Colonialism, globalization, modernity, and monoculturalism have amplified mistrust and enmity among different ethnic groups, genders, social classes, and nationalities. We have become victims of global monoculturalism, experiencing tribalism, nationalism, and environmental destruction. Tribalism and nationalism create divisions and hierarchies based on heteropatriarchal racial normativity, fostering an "us-versus-them" mentality that goes against the inclusive nature of Christ's love. Environmental destruction, driven by greed and disregard for God's creation, endangers our planet and the well-being of future generations.

Probiotic Theology and Conviviality

I am recently thinking of a different metaphor for practical theology (PT) as an experience-reflection-praxis mode of training for ministry and missions. I am calling it probiotic theology (as opposed to antibiotic theology). It is rooted in John 14 and the praxis of Jesus as the way, the truth, and the life of the world.

For the last five hundred years we have operated with an antibiotic approach to theology whereby evangelizing, preaching, and pastoring has meant wounding and exterminating entire communities that look different, think differently, and worship differently. Probiotic theology reverses the effect of the gospel of extermination back into a gospel of life, and life abundant. Probiotic theology plays a critical role in helping us commit to intercultural, interfaith, and interpolitical dialogue, essential for embodying conviviality. It encourages us to apply our faith in tangible ways, fostering understanding and collaboration across cultural, religious, and political divides. By engaging in intercultural dialogue, we appreciate the richness of diverse cultures and perspectives.

Probiotic theology urges us to see the image of God in every person and culture, breaking down prejudices and fostering mutual respect. This aligns with the Christian mandate to love our neighbors, regardless of their cultural background, gender and sexual identities, and geographical locations.

Probiotic theology encourages interfaith dialogue, promoting peace and understanding between different religious communities. By focusing on common values and shared goals, we can address global challenges such as poverty, injustice, antisemitism, Islamophobia, and environmental degradation. Interfaith dialogue helps build bridges of understanding and cooperation, reflecting the inclusive love of Christ through praxis rather than conversionist postures—making them like us but not really!

Engaging in interpolitical dialogue is crucial for addressing the deep-seated divisions in our societies. Probiotic theology teaches us to approach political differences with humility and a commitment to the shared good—well-living. By fostering respectful conversations and seeking mutual ground, we can work towards policies that benefit the vibrant diversity of society, promoting justice and equity.

Hope for Global Conviviality in Christ's Spirit

Jesus's message is rooted in Jesus's praxis (Christopraxis) of coming together in his unconditional and decolonial love. He came to break down the walls of hostility and unite us in his love. The church, as the body of Christ, is called to be a beacon of hope and a model of community living against the structures of oppression, tribalism, nationalism, and ecocide. We must strive to create spaces of communion, dialogue, and shared life, where people from diverse backgrounds can come together and find common ground in Christopraxis. We may not agree on dogmas and sometimes feel disappointed with our tradition's histories, but we can agree on the life-giving conditions needed to sustain our devastated communities, which, like the Crucified One, are calling us to a decolonial love often against our religious traditions.

In confronting tribalism and nationalism, we should emphasize our shared humanity and the common goal of living in peace and harmony. By promoting intercultural translation and world cooperation, we can work towards a "pluri-versal" global community (a world where many worlds fit). Similarly, addressing environmental destruction requires us to recognize our vulnerability as creatures cared for by Mother Earth and our responsibility as stewards of God's creation. We must adopt sustainable practices and advocate for policies that protect the environment and promote the well-being of all living creatures even if the consequence is persecution. This is not "something else" apart from the gospel; it is a sacred mission of the gospel of life.

Centering Thought

In a divided and distrustful world, we are called to rediscover the joy of life together, our shared humanity. As relational beings, we thrive in mutual care and dialogue, yet forces like colonialism, nationalism, and individualism fracture our bonds. Through Christ-centered probiotic theology, we affirm God's image in every person, fostering respect, justice, and sustainability. In Christ's Spirit, we strive for a vibrant variety united in love and flourishing together.

Prayer

Jesus, heal my social dysfunctionality,
my antibiotic theology . . .
Jesus, make me like you!
Make me a person with the desire to live life
with others in decolonial love.
Help me to overcome personal mistrust
and embody global conviviality,
fostering shared vulnerability and responsibility for creation.

Personal Journal Prompts

- Reflect on past negative experiences with others. How have these experiences contributed to your sense of mistrust?
- What does it mean to you to live with others for Jesus's sake? How does this influence your daily interactions?
- When sharing the good news with people from different backgrounds, do you focus on similarities or differences? How do you balance the word of God with the work of God in these relationships?
- How can you actively contribute to overcoming tribalism, nationalism, and environmental destruction within your community?

Day 18

Temptation

Scripture

No testing has overtaken you that is not common to everyone. God is faithful, and he will not let you be tested beyond your strength, but with the testing he will also provide the way out so that you may be able to endure it.

—1 Corinthians 10:13

Understanding Temptation

Temptation is an unavoidable part of life. Instead of seeking to escape it, we should strive to understand its purpose as we grow and develop. Temptation often brings us into critical moments marked by anxiety and self-reflection. These periods offer profound opportunities for discovery—about ourselves, those around us, and God.

Temptation is neither inherently positive nor negative. It functions as a mirror, revealing our weaknesses (vices) and strengths (virtues). Because it exposes us so fully, we often view temptation negatively, as it forces us to confront areas we'd rather avoid.

The Transformative Nature of Temptation

From a biblical perspective, God uses trials and temptations as tools for education and transformation (Job). Temptation pushes us to the edge of our human tolerance, allowing us to see ourselves more clearly (Abraham and Sara). It reveals how well—or poorly—we can manage challenging situations and relationships (David).

Often, temptation brings us face-to-face with our fears or discomforts, things we might otherwise avoid (Jesus of Nazareth). Through these trials, we learn to appreciate what truly matters, especially the things we lack during such moments. These experiences teach us that God is greater than any possession, pleasure, or dread.

Temptation also highlights the pleasures and addictions that bind us emotionally or physically (Ananias and Saphira). If we give in, we discover the extent of our dependencies; if we resist, we uncover new strength and freedom. In the hands of God, any temptation—no matter how painful—can lead to transformation (Amma Syncletica).[26]

Christ as a Way to Face Temptations

In Jesus Christ, we see the ultimate example of perseverance through temptation. He faced temptation throughout his earthly life, enduring suffering and trials while remaining obedient to God. Through his perseverance, Jesus overcame the greatest enemies: the tempter, human deception, and death.

In Christ, we learn to endure and emerge victorious from temptation, becoming courageous, disciplined, and resilient. Discipleship means daily self-denial, carrying our cross, and moving forward with faith in God and community. Any notion of a life *free from* temptation is neither Christian nor realistic—it is both naive and dangerous.

World Wisdom

Temptation, as a universal human experience, has been explored across cultures and traditions. In Buddhism, the concept of *māra* represents the internal and external forces that distract us from enlightenment, emphasizing mindfulness and discipline as paths to overcoming temptation. In Stoic philosophy, figures like Epictetus and Marcus Aurelius teach the importance of self-control and inner resilience in the face of external challenges.

These perspectives align with the Christian understanding that temptation is not something to dread but an opportunity for growth. By recognizing its presence and confronting it with wisdom, we develop virtues that align us with God's will and purpose until renewal.

Living Through Temptation

Temptation is not meant to be evaded but endured with perseverance. It is a tool for spiritual and emotional growth, revealing the areas of our lives that need healing, discipline, and transformation. As we face temptation, we are called to rely on God's faithfulness and the support of a mature community, trusting that God and community will provide the strength and the way to overcome.

By viewing temptation as an opportunity rather than a threat, we shift our mindset from avoidance to engagement. This perspective allows us to grow in self-awareness and deepen our dependence on God and interdependence with community, discovering the Spirit's grace and power in our weakness.

Centering Thought

Temptation is a universal experience, but in Christ, it becomes a pathway to transformation. By enduring temptation with faith and perseverance in community, we discover greater freedom, deeper wisdom, and a stronger connection to God's purpose for our lives.

Prayer

Jesus, make me like you!
Make me a person resilient through temptation.
Teach me to embrace the challenges of life
with faith, courage, and perseverance.
Help me to recognize your presence, through community, in my trials
and to trust in your strength to overcome.

Personal Journal Prompts

- What periods of testing have shaped your life? How have they helped you grow? Write a timeline.

- How do you usually react when faced with temptation? Flight, fight or hide? Are there patterns you've noticed?

- In what ways does Jesus help you resist temptation day by day? What is the role of community when you face trials?

Day 19

Words of Life and Words of Death

Scripture

Indeed, the word of God is living and active and sharper than any two-edged sword, piercing until it divides soul from spirit, joints from marrow; it is able to judge the thoughts and intentions of the heart.

—Hebrews 4:12 NRSVue

The Power of Words

WORDS ARE POWERFUL, NOT because they are inherently magical or objective but because they carry our deepest desires and intentions. This was one of the basic teachings of Jesus: "What defiles a person is not what goes into the mouth; it is what comes out of the mouth that defiles a person. . . . For out of the heart come evil ideas, murder, adultery, sexual immorality, theft, false testimony, slander" (Matt 15:11, 19 NET).

The meaning of words, as the Austrian-British philosopher Ludwig Wittgenstein emphasized, is shaped by their use in language.[27] There are words that encourage and bring life, and others that discourage and inspire death. Every word that comes out of our mouths is personal, as we are the ones who give them birth.

There are also empty words because there are empty and unhappy people. Silence is not necessarily the opposite of words; there are silences that say a lot (as in the case of Jesus in front of Pilate) and wordiness that says little (as illustrated in the parable of the Pharisee and the tax collector in the temple).

Word of Life

Jesus Christ is the enfleshed divine Word, the Logos (Living Word). Jesus Christ is the Word that says it all, the Word of life, the fully expressed divine intention that gives meaning to our humanity, the living Word of God that makes us living beings. Jesus Christ came as the Word of life, grace, and reconciliation. In Jesus Christ, we find the breath of life and learn to speak words of life, grace, and *shalom*.

The mouth is not the primary organ of the Word of life, but faith, which places us within the living Word and teaches us to speak words ingrained in life that release more words of well-living. Jesus Christ came to teach us new words, the ones he heard from his Father and transmits to us through his Spirit: "I am the way and the truth and the life. No one comes to the Father except through me" (John 14:6 NRSVue).

Terminal Knowledge

Human knowledge is a social construction deeply intertwined with power structures, argues the Portuguese political scholar Boaventura de Sousa Santos.[28] "Evil ideas" beget terminal (deathly) knowledge that constructs deathly imperial structures. Christianity was born within the womb of terminal knowledge and deathly imperial structures (Roman imperial coloniality). "Jesus, the Lord" became the new idea, in the form of the earliest Christian confession, that gave birth to healing knowledge from within the structures sustaining terminal (deathly) knowledge.

In the early stages of Christianity, whoever confessed and propagated this new word—"Jesus, the Lord"—would be captured, sentenced, and cruelly executed in front of an imperial audience that celebrated deathly power structures as a spectacle. However, the moment when the Christian religion became part of the imperial power structure, the new word of the kingdom became subjected to the old word of the empire, and confusion propagated across the centuries.

Word of Death

We live today in a complicated context where we no longer know with clarity what is the word of God and the word of empire. According to the renowned Swiss pastor and theologian Karl Barth, we resemble today the time of the tower of Babel (Gen 11) in our modern daily life, a time when the righteousness of the state, the righteousness of the law, the righteousness of businesses, and even the righteousness of the church are confused with the righteousness of God. "Are we not, with our religious righteousness, acting 'as if'—in order not to have to deal with reality? Is not our religious righteousness a product of our pride and our despair, a tower of Babel, at which the devil laughs more loudly than at all the others?"[29] If Barth were alive today, he would further emphasize, "the devil laughs [even] more loudly."

New Words in the Spirit

The words we choose and the meanings we attach to them can either reinforce or challenge these imperial power structures. Becoming a follower of Jesus Christ requires, nowadays, unlearning the false meanings of righteousness and relearning to speak new words in the power of the Spirit of the resurrected Lord until we develop the new language of grace.

The word of self-righteousness and condemnation is the old word, which bound and silenced us while we lived religiously and morally against Jesus Christ. It is the same word that condemned and brought Jesus Christ to the cross of Calvary. A committed follower of Jesus Christ does not speak words of condemnation but words of compassion, repentance, peace, and hope. The words that come from those who are constantly abiding in the Word of life are words that attract, give purpose, dismantle imperial structures, and heal hearts broken by words of condemnation. The life of the believer can be summarized in one word: Jesus Christ, the Lord!

Centering Thought

Words have the power to create or destroy, liberate or oppress. In Jesus Christ, the living Word, we find life, grace, and renewal. Yet, human words often generate and also mirror systems of domination and death. As followers of Christ, we are called to unlearn self-righteousness and condemnation, speaking instead words of life with compassion, hope, and healing. Let our lives proclaim the ultimate word—Jesus Christ, the Lord!—a confession that dismantles oppression and embody God's kingdom of peace and justice

Prayer

Jesus Christ, the Lord, free us from false righteousness
and a life without compassion.
Jesus, make me like you!
Make me a person who transmits words of life.

Personal Journal Prompts

- Reflect on a time when you felt the weight of condemnation. How did these words affect your self-perception and your relationship with others?

Words of Life and Words of Death

- Consider a moment when a word of life and grace transformed you. What was this word, and how did it change your outlook or behavior?

- Identify any words of condemnation or self-righteousness that you might still hold in your personal vocabulary. Make a list. How can you replace these with words of compassion, renewal, and hope? Write down alternatives.

- Think about the power structures that influence your understanding of righteousness. How can you challenge these structures by adopting the language of Jesus, the Living Word?

Day 20

Mother

Scripture

*When Jesus saw his mother and the disciple
whom he loved standing beside her,
he said to his mother, "Woman, here is your son."
Then he said to the disciple, "Here is your mother."
And from that hour the disciple took her into his own home.*

—John 19:26–27

The Maternal Presence

THE MATERNAL PRESENCE, IN any form, is indispensable for our well-being and happiness. The figure of "mother" holds a sacred place in our hearts—filled for some with beautiful memories and for others with deep longing or lament. A popular national hymn in my home country declares, "In the name of mother lies the greatest expression of love," capturing its profound emotional resonance.

The word "mother" evokes thoughts of origin, care, affection, forgiveness, sacrifice, tolerance, resilience, and dignity. So essential is the maternal connection that when life denies us a mother, we often seek maternal figures elsewhere, adopting mothers as naturally as children are adopted.

The Maternal Nature of God

Theologically, God as Creator is also Sustainer, embodying both paternal and maternal qualities. For those who struggle to relate to God as "Father," the metaphor of "Mother" can offer a profound connection. God's nature transcends human gender categories, encompassing the nurturing, protective, and sustaining aspects we associate with motherhood.

In Christian feminist and *mujerista* theology, this maternal imagery of God takes on a liberative dimension. It emphasizes God as a source of life and sustenance, particularly for those who are marginalized or oppressed. Womanist theologians highlight how maternal qualities—such as resilience, self-sacrifice, and unconditional love—mirror the divine character, challenging patriarchal structures that limit the fullness of God's presence.

Our earthly mothers are reflections of this divine maternal love. While they are not without fault, they serve as tangible expressions of God's nurturing care, sustaining life, offering comfort, and guiding us toward wholeness. For those without a maternal figure, God's maternal presence remains accessible through the relationships and communities that embody divine care.

Mary: A Maternal Witness

Jesus's relationship with Mary highlights the importance of the maternal presence in salvation history. Mary's role as the mother of Jesus extends beyond biological motherhood; she is a key figure in the Christian story, demonstrating faith, courage, and leadership. Her presence in the early church, as seen in Acts and the Gospels, reveals her as a spiritual mother to the community of believers.

In Christ, we learn to see the maternal nature of God. Mary's love for Jesus and her role in the church inspire mothers to reflect God's presence in their relationships with their children and with the "social orphans" entrusted to them. This call extends beyond biological motherhood to all who nurture, guide, and sustain others in love and faith.

Through popular religion, Mary as the sacred metaphor of Divine Motherhood becomes a living and dynamic presence in the lives of people worldwide. Her veneration transcends doctrinal boundaries, rooted in everyday practices, cultural expressions, and personal devotion. Rosary prayers, pilgrimages, and festivals devoted to Our Lady of Guadalupe and La Virgen de Suyapa (Latin America), Virgen de Fátima (Portugal), and the festival of Flores de Mayo (Philippines) are communal expressions of faith that reinforce people's communal bonds with the maternal dimension of God.

The Maternal Call in a Broken World

In a world marked by abandonment, disconnection, and social orphanhood, the maternal presence is a healing force. Christian feminist perspectives emphasize the need for communities to embody maternal care, creating spaces of inclusion, refuge, and restoration. *Mujerista* theology, rooted in the experiences of Latina women, calls for a spirituality that nurtures life in the face of systemic oppression, honoring the sacredness of motherhood as a communal and liberating force.

The maternal call is not confined to gender. All who follow Christ are invited to embody maternal care, protecting the vulnerable, advocating for justice, and nurturing life in all its forms. To embrace the maternal nature of God is to participate in the divine work of sustaining and renewing creation.

Centering Thought

The maternal presence, whether through our earthly mothers or the sacred or the divine nature of God, is a profound gift that sustains life and reflects God's unconditional love. By embracing this presence, we honor God's nurturing care and participate in the sacred and resilient work of creating, restoring, and sustaining life in a broken world.

Prayer

Jesus, make me like you!
Make me a child who sees the divine presence
through the gift of a mother, material and symbolic,
and a caregiver who reflects God's love
to those entrusted to my care.

Personal Journal Prompts

- If you are a mother, how do you express God's love and care to your children?
- What role has your mother played in your life? If you didn't know her, who have you adopted as a mother figure and why?
- What does the relationship between Jesus and Mary teach you about God's maternal presence and how you can reflect it in your life?

Day 21

Abba Father and Social Orphanhood

Scripture

For you did not receive a spirit of slavery to fall back into fear, but you have received a spirit of adoption. When we cry, "Abba! Father!" it is that very Spirit bearing witness with our spirit that we are children of God.

—ROMANS 8:15–16

Abba Father

ANYONE WHO HAS A loving and virtuous father possesses a priceless treasure. The absence of such a figure in our lives leads to immeasurable human poverty. We all need a father figure to be truly happy. The alarming absence of fathers in many of our families brings devastating social consequences. If the name "mother" encapsulates the greatest expression of love, the name "father" encapsulates wisdom, stability, and protection.

Henri Nouwen, a renowned spiritual writer, highlighted the profound issue of spiritual and societal orphanhood in America.

He observed that many individuals, even those with living parents, experience a deep sense of abandonment and lack of guidance, leading to a spiritual void. This orphanhood is not only a personal crisis but a societal one, affecting community structures and personal development.[30]

Healthy emotional attachment to a father figure is crucial for our development. It cultivates a sense of security, self-worth, and emotional resilience. Conversely, a bad or absent attachment can lead to emotional instability, a lack of self-esteem, and difficulties in forming healthy relationships. The void left by a missing father figure can be deeply felt and may manifest in various detrimental behaviors and attitudes. Research has shown that these effects are even more pronounced in the Majority World, where economic and social challenges exacerbate the impact of father absence in the family system due to premature death, migration, additions, and domestic violence. Studies indicate that children in these regions suffer more severe psychological and developmental setbacks when deprived of a stable father figure compared to their counterparts in Western societies which tend to be more individualistically wired.

Indigenous Wisdom and Healing

Indigenous cultures offer valuable insights into healing father attachment disorders. They emphasize the importance of ancestry, cultural modeling, and ancient wisdom. Ancestral teachings and cultural practices provide a framework for understanding one's place in the world, fostering a sense of identity and belonging. Indigenous communities often engage in rituals and storytelling that reinforce the values and lessons passed down through generations, helping to heal the wounds caused by father absence. These practices highlight the collective responsibility of the community in raising and nurturing children, ensuring that the role of a father is supplemented by a network of supportive relationships.

The Role of God as Father

God, in his role as a spiritual father (source of love and life), often comes to fill the empty spaces of a generation orphaned by fathers. One of the greatest revelations made by Jesus Christ is showing us the fatherly character of God. God is a merciful and just Father, jovial and joyful, patient and forgiving, who corrects those he loves and provides equally for his good and bad children. In Jesus Christ, we find the beautiful relationship of Abba (Daddy), which denotes great trust and intimacy. Through Jesus Christ, we confidently come to God as our Abba.

The Role of the Father in Society

From reading Scripture today, we can conclude that God is seeking fathers after God's own heart. Our communities need social fathers, progenitors of healthy models of family, church, and society. Cultural fathers play an essential role in shaping culture; they are pillars of civic and political life who model life-giving order and contribute to the future of society through effort, morality, and example. Our cities need civic fathers who are committed to good living principles, and our churches need servant fathers who take on their roles as spiritual leaders, husbands, and mentors of generational change.

Surviving Evil, Patriarchal, Immoral Fatherhood

In many cases, all these roles seem aspirational rather than realistic. How do we survive as world societies in orphanhood without loving servant fathers? How do we survive the horror of patriarchal violent fatherhood? What about the deception of male supremacy stealing God's father identity to use it as a legitimizing mechanism for self-entitlement, self-satisfaction, immorality, and age-gender subjugation?

The words of Jesus to his own generation and context, in the Gospel of John, is also applicable to our world and time of orphanhood and imperial, patriarchal, immoral fatherhood today: "They said to him therefore, 'Where is your Father?' Jesus answered, 'You know neither me nor my Father. If you knew me, you would know my Father also. . . . Why do you not understand what I say? It is because you cannot bear to hear my word. You are of your father the devil, and your will is to do your father's desires. He was a murderer from the beginning, and does not stand in the truth, because there is no truth in him. When he lies, he speaks out of his own character, for he is a liar and the father of lies" (John 8:19, 43–44 ESV).

Fatherhood is more than mere maleness! And when maleness becomes a tool of oppression, immorality, and violence, God reroutes sacred fatherhood through other means: mothers, Godmothers, sisters, mentors, and other caretakers at the service of God's love and life.

Centering Thought

Spiritual support is fundamental in nurturing a healthy father-child relationship beyond maleness. The church provides a community where spiritual fathers can offer guidance, love, and mentorship. Cultural support also plays a significant role. Societal values that promote strong family structures and fatherhood are essential in reinforcing the importance of a father's role.

Prayer

Jesus, heal me from the consequences
of evil patriarchal fatherhood.
Jesus, make me like you!
Make me someone who fathers people and generations
according to God's love!

Personal Journal Prompts

- Reflect on what comes to mind when you think of your father. How has this shaped your understanding of fatherhood?
- Consider the presence of spiritual orphans around you. Are you in a position to offer guidance and support? Are you one of them?
- How does the Abba Father relationship of Jesus Christ inspire you to seek God's fatherhood and imitate it for someone who sees you as a father figure?

Day 22

Tomorrow

Scripture

Therefore, I tell you, do not worry about your life, what you will eat or what you will drink, or about your body, what you will wear. Is not life more than food, and the body more than clothing? . . . But strive first for the kingdom of God and his righteousness, and all these things will be given to you as well. So do not worry about tomorrow, for tomorrow will bring worries of its own. Today's trouble is enough for today.

—Matthew 6:25, 33–34

Time and Mortality

To live peacefully with time is to embrace one of the greatest challenges of being human. Time relentlessly reminds us of our mortality, a reality many of us evade. Death, the ultimate boundary of human existence, is feared and avoided through constant distraction. Some of us bury ourselves in work, entertainment, or endless busyness, while others invest heavily in appearances, hoping to stave off aging. Even ministry, meant to be a labor of hope, can become an escape from facing our limits.

Modern science and technology feed this illusion. In a world of rapid innovation, many hold on to the dream of defeating death altogether, imagining immortality as a scientific breakthrough. Time is seen as an adversary, pressing the wealthy to secure their power and the marginalized to search for survival. Yet no matter how we fight or ignore it, time remains beyond our control, an ever-present reminder of our finitude. As Ecclesiastes laments, "Vanity of vanities . . . everything is striving after the wind" (1:11).

Jesus Christ: The Lord of Tomorrow

In *Theology of Hope*, Jürgen Moltmann reminds us that Christian faith is deeply oriented toward the future, not as a distant abstraction but as the living promise of God breaking into the present. Jesus Christ, the firstborn of the resurrection, embodies this promise. He is the Lord of time—the Alpha and Omega—who overcame death and opened the path to abundant life, here and beyond.

In Jesus Christ, we find the person of tomorrow who meets us today, transforming our relationship with time. As Justo González explores in *Mañana: Christian Theology from a Hispanic Perspective*, this promise of tomorrow is not merely individual but communal.[31] It is a future of justice, restoration, and wholeness for all creation. To follow Christ is to live as people of tomorrow, embracing hope and participating in the unfolding of God's kingdom here and now and with creation.

Time, often experienced as an oppressive force, becomes in Jesus Christ a servant of God's cosmic purposes. For those who walk with the Spirit, time pushes us forward when we falter and holds us back when we are at risk of falling. Time becomes an ally, leading us toward the fullness of life promised in Christ. Tomorrow is no longer a threat but a gift—a *kairos*; a favorable time in God's redemptive plan, one already planted and yet to come: "For I am convinced that neither death nor life, neither angels nor demons, neither the present nor the future, nor any powers, neither height nor depth, nor anything else in all creation, will be able to separate us from the love of God that is in Christ Jesus our Lord" (Rom 8:38–39 NIV).

Living as People of Tomorrow

To live as people of tomorrow is to let go of the anxiety that binds us to today. It is to trust in God's provision, knowing that time itself belongs to the Creator. This is not a call to passive waiting but to active hope, rooted in the assurance that God's future is breaking into the present.

Christian feminist and liberation theologians emphasize that living into tomorrow requires attentiveness to present realities of oppression and injustice. Tomorrow is not only about individual salvation but about the collective hope for a just and equitable world. It invites us to embody the values of God's kingdom—mercy, justice, and reconciliation—in our daily lives.

World religions also offer profound insights into living in harmony with time. In Buddhism, the concept of impermanence (*anicca*) teaches us to accept the transitory nature of life without fear or attachment. This mindfulness toward the present moment resonates with the Christian call to seek God's kingdom in the here and now while holding an eternal perspective. Similarly, Hinduism's cyclical view of time encourages us to see tomorrow not as a finite endpoint but as part of a continuous journey of growth, renewal, and ultimate union with the divine. These perspectives remind us to live fully in the present while remaining attuned to the sacred rhythms of life.

Indigenous traditions often perceive time not as linear but as circular, interconnected, and relational. In many Indigenous cultures, tomorrow is tied to the continuity of life within the natural world and the wisdom of ancestors. Living as people of tomorrow means honoring these connections, understanding that our actions today shape the future for generations to come. This perspective aligns with the biblical understanding of stewardship and care for creation, emphasizing our responsibility to live harmoniously with the Earth and each other.

Incorporating these perspectives, living as people of tomorrow calls us to a holistic approach to time. It is an invitation to align our actions with God's purposes, honoring the sacredness of time as a gift. By embracing the wisdom of diverse traditions, we learn to walk humbly, hope boldly, and work collectively toward the flourishing of all creation. Tomorrow, seen through this lens, becomes a shared promise of justice, renewal, and reconciliation.

Centering Thought

To live in peace with time is to embrace the hope of Christ's resurrection and new creation. In Christ's Spirit, we are freed from the fear of death and empowered to live each day with purpose, trusting in the promise of a future that is both already here and yet to come. It is a life that not only has a past (tradition) or holds to the present (mission) but yearns for the future (imagination) as a walk with the Spirit of life. This is the gift of tomorrow: not merely a distant horizon but a living hope that transforms the present.

Prayer

Jesus, make me like you!
Make me a person of tomorrow,
living with hope and purpose today.
Teach me to walk in your time,
trusting in your provision
and building your kingdom each day.

Personal Journal Prompts

- How do you currently live in relation to time? Do you ignore it, fight it, or embrace it?

Tomorrow

- What do you expect of tomorrow? How does your vision of the future shape who you are today? What is the role of the Spirit of God in that vision?
- In what ways does Jesus Christ inspire you to live into God's tomorrow?

Day 23

Gratitude
Grace as an Alternative to Meanness

Scripture

*Give thanks in all circumstances;
for this is the will of God in Christ Jesus for you.*

—1 THESSALONIANS 5:18

*The law was brought in so that the trespass might increase.
But where sin increased, grace increased all the more.*

—ROMANS 5:20 NIV

The Nature of Gratitude

HAPPINESS IS IMPOSSIBLE WITHOUT gratitude. Gratitude is a hallmark of emotionally healthy people, while its opposite—ingratitude—leads to a distorted view of the world. The ungrateful see life through the lens of disgrace, perceiving existence as hostile, competitive, and dominated by envy and self-merit.

Ungrateful pessimists live in a cycle of victimization, believing they are owed assistance because of their perceived suffering. Conversely, ungrateful optimists see themselves narcissistically as self-made and deserving of their achievements, acknowledging no one else's contribution. Both live apart from grace, trapped in cycles of entitlement and alienation.

At its core, gratitude flows from grace—the recognition of life and opportunity as an unearned gift. To be grateful is to understand that we are sustained by the unmerited goodness of God. Grateful people recognize God as their provider and strength, responding to life's challenges and blessings with contentment and trust. As Phil 4:11–12 reminds us, true gratitude is not tied to abundance or scarcity but rooted in the giver of grace, whose sufficiency transcends circumstances.

Meanness as an Obstacle to Gratitude

In polarized times like ours, meanness thrives, co-opting gratitude and grace. Meanness emerges as a defensive posture against perceived threats, fueled by entitlement, pride, or fear. It polarizes relationships and societies, turning potential connections into hostile divides. Meanness poisons gratitude by cultivating a spirit of scarcity: "What I have is mine because I earned it," or, "What I lack is someone else's fault."

Gratitude, in contrast, disrupts meanness. It reorients us to abundance, reminding us that life is a gift, not a competition. To live gratefully is to practice spiritual activism—choosing to resist the toxicity of entitlement and hostility by actively acknowledging the grace present in our lives and extending it to others.

Gratitude as Spiritual Activism

Gratitude is more than a feeling; it is a practice, a discipline, and a transformative force. By choosing gratitude, we shift from scarcity to abundance, from entitlement to humility, and from isolation to community. This spiritual activism becomes a witness in a fractured world, modeling the grace of God that transcends divisions.

In many religious traditions, gratitude is foundational to spiritual growth. Buddhist teachings emphasize mindfulness of the present moment as a source of gratitude, while Indigenous spiritualities often center gratitude as a way of life, honoring the interconnectedness of creation. These perspectives align with the Christian understanding that gratitude is a response to God's grace—a posture of openness and humility that fosters harmony with God, others, and creation.

Gratitude in Christ

Jesus Christ is the ultimate gift of God's grace to creation, the greatest reason for gratitude. In Christ, we see grace embodied—God with us and for us. In the power of the Spirit, Jesus lived a life of gratitude, even in the face of rejection and suffering. On the cross, he bore humanity's ingratitude and transformed it into grace, offering us the opportunity to live abundantly in him. This is Jesus's mission statement: to offer abundant life to all (John 10:10)

To follow Christ is to live in gratitude, recognizing that we are called to extend that grace to others. In Christ, gratitude becomes a pathway to growth, abundance, and joy, shaping us into people who reflect God's generosity in a world marked by scarcity and division.

Centering Thought

Gratitude is the antidote to meanness and division, a spiritual discipline that reconnects us to God's grace and abundance. In Christ, by the power of the Spirit, we learn to live in gratitude, transforming our lives and the lives of others through the simple yet profound recognition that everything we have is a gift.

GRATITUDE

Prayer

Jesus, make me like you!
Make me a person filled with gratitude and grace,
freed from meanness and entitlement.
Teach me to live abundantly in power of the Spirit,
and share your goodness with others.

Personal Journal Prompts

- Do you consider yourself a grateful or ungrateful person? Reflect on why. Check with friends and family about this.
- Make a list of reasons you have to give thanks and to lament.
- What acts of kindness can you extend to others as a reflection of your thankfulness? Likewise, what acts of kindness are others extending to you that you may not be acknowledging?
- If your vocation were to become a disrupter of meanness through gratitude, where would you start?

Day 24

Redemption and Abandonment

Scripture

For the Son of Man came not to be served but to serve, and to give his life a ransom for many.

—MARK 10:45

The Need for Redemption

WE ALL NEED TO be redeemed to find happiness. At its core, redemption is an act of profound love. True love does not abandon easily; instead, it seeks to rescue and restore at any cost. Abandonment, like betrayal, is one of the most devastating human experiences because it comes from those we trust and rely on. To be abandoned is to feel devalued, betrayed, purposeless, and hopeless—sometimes to the point of despair or even death.

Abandonment is not only personal but also societal. War, for instance, starkly reveals who is protected and who is deemed expendable, which lives are considered more worthy than others. In our time, with over fifty nations embroiled in armed conflict—the highest number since 1946—this disparity is painfully evident.[32] Nowhere is this clearer than in the ongoing war in Gaza since October 7, 2023.

Rethinking Redemption After Gaza

We cannot find words to express the excruciating pain of Israeli families whose relatives were kidnapped and held hostage by the criminal acts of the Izz al-Din al-Qassam Brigades. Yet, there are also no words to adequately describe the horror in Gaza—the Palestinian genocide carried out by the State of Israel under Prime Minister Netanyahu.

A dear Palestinian Christian pastor and theologian shared with me that the primary lament for Palestinians in this dark time is not a sense of God's absence. They feel God is with them in their misery. Their lament is for humanity's abandonment of them, particularly the complicity and silence of the global evangelical church.

How can we speak of redemption and peace in a context of such complicit extermination? Before the church can be received as a redemptive community, it must first become a repentant and redeemed community. Living redemptively begins with the confession of allegiance to violence, complicity in systems of oppression, and the deliberate turning away from these sins toward justice and restoration. And this is a "costly" price, to quote Dietrich Bonhoeffer.[33]

Christ as the Redeemer

Redemption is the embodiment of God's unwavering love, a public witness of restoration and liberation in the face of hate, violence, and oppression. In Christ, redemption is not merely a private or spiritual transaction but a bold act of love that confronts systems of imperial violence, cultivates shalom amidst chaos, and proclaims freedom for those in sociopolitical and existential captivity. Jesus Christ bore the ultimate agony of abandonment, crying out, "My

God, my God, why have you forsaken me?" (Mark 15:34). And in doing that, we were embraced by him as a community in constant redemption.

To live as redeemed and redemptive people is to embody this love through actions that bridge divisions, restore broken relationships, and resist the forces of dehumanization. Let us be agents of redemption, bearing witness to justice, peace, and grace in a world desperate for transformation.

Redemption in a Time of War and Injustice

In contexts of war and systemic violence, redemption requires more than abstract theological reflection. It demands concrete acts of repentance and solidarity. To live redemptively is to stand against systems that perpetuate violence and to prioritize the lives of those the world deems unworthy.

The church, as a redemptive community, must embody the grace and justice of Christ historically. This begins with lament and repentance, confessing our complicity in violence—whether through silence, inaction, or active support of oppressive powers. Living redemptively requires speaking out against injustice, advocating for the oppressed, and working toward reconciliation and peace.

A theology of redemption also calls us to learn from Indigenous wisdom and practices of just peacemaking. Many Indigenous traditions emphasize the interconnectedness of all life and the necessity of restorative justice. Redemption, in this sense, is not only about individual salvation but about the healing of communities and creation. Indigenous frameworks teach us the importance of ceremonies of forgiveness, practices of mutual care, and the sacred responsibility to protect life. These lessons are indispensable for the church's witness in a broken world.

Redemption and Healing

From the perspective of clinical psychology, abandonment leaves deep emotional scars that often manifest as attachment disorders, anxiety, or depression. Healing from abandonment involves rebuilding trust, restoring relationships, and fostering environments of safety and care. The Christian call to redemption aligns with this psychological insight: it is an act of restoration that affirms human worth and cultivates connection.

In Jesus Christ, redemption is personal, communal, and cosmic. The church, as his body, is called to be a redemptive community—a place where the abandoned are welcomed, the broken are restored, and the wounded are healed. This involves living out a redemptive ethic in how we treat one another, bearing witness to Christ's sacrificial love.

Living Redemptively

Living redemptively means becoming redeemed agents of restoration in a world marked by abandonment and estrangement. It is a commitment to walk alongside those in pain, offering hope and presence as Christ does for us. This includes resisting the allure of violence, embracing just peacemaking, and learning from those who have long practiced the art of communal healing.

Centering Thought

Redemption is the essence of God's love, a relentless pursuit of restoration and healing. In Christ, we are called to live as redeemed and redemptive people, transforming abandonment into communion, despair into hope, and estrangement into belonging. Let us repent and be agents of redemption in a world longing for justice, peace, and grace.

Prayer

Jesus, make me like you!
Make me a person who embodies redemptive love,
confessing where I have failed
and committing to acts of restoration,
offering grace and healing to the abandoned and oppressed.

Personal Journal Prompts

- Have you ever felt abandoned? How did it shape your understanding of trust and love?
- In what ways have you been complicit in systems of abandonment or violence? What steps can you take to repent?
- What acts of redemption—toward individuals, communities, or creation—can you incorporate into your life?

Day 25

Devotional Life
Starting the Day with Sacred Intention

Scripture

O Lord, in the morning you hear my voice;
in the morning I plead my case to you and watch.

—Psalm 5:3

Satisfy us in the morning with your steadfast love,
so that we may rejoice and be glad all our days.

—Psalm 90:14

Devotion as Sacred Rhythm

SETTING ASIDE DAILY TIME to meditate on God and our life is essential for a purposeful and fulfilling existence. Well-being in daily life requires sacred spaces woven into the fabric of our routines. These moments remind us that God is present in every aspect of life, infusing the ordinary with divine purpose. To live without this awareness is to wander aimlessly, vulnerable to the demands and agendas of "other gods"—those forces that enslave us without our realizing it.

In the Judeo-Christian tradition, the Sabbath (*shabbat*) is a sacred day of rest and renewal, a divine gift that integrates time and eternity. Abraham J. Heschel, in his profound reflections on the Sabbath, describes it as a "sanctuary in time."[34] Unlike spaces that are built and possessed, the Sabbath creates a holy architecture of time, inviting us to step out of the tyranny of the urgent and into the eternal rhythm of grace. A devotional practice can be understood as a "daily Sabbath," a sacred pause amidst the busy-ness of life.

Each morning, like the Sabbath, is an opportunity to recognize time as a gift, a reminder that God is not bound by human constructs of productivity. The rhythms of each day, the cycles of seasons—all carry divine significance, signaling God's presence and desire to renew us. Heschel notes that "the meaning of the Sabbath is to celebrate time rather than space,"[35] inviting us to consecrate not just the seventh day but every moment of life. Morning devotion aligns us with this sanctified rhythm, marking our day with purpose, gratitude, and hope.

The Daily Rhythm of Renewal

Jesus Christ inaugurated the "favorable day of the Lord" (Luke 4:19), a perpetual invitation to live each day as a gift of grace. In Christ, each morning becomes an opportunity to embrace life with courage, purpose, and resilience. Starting the day with Christ transforms it from a struggle for survival into an act of co-creation with God.

Henri Nouwen and Thomas Merton remind us that a devotional life is not about achieving perfection but about cultivating awareness. Nouwen points us to devotional time as a way to move from *busy-ness* to *presence*, from *fear* to *love*.[36] Similarly, Merton's emphasis on solitude and contemplation invites us to listen deeply, not just to God but to the rhythms of our own lives.[37]

In Indigenous spiritualities, the dawn is a sacred moment of renewal. Morning rituals often involve gratitude for the new day, acknowledgment of the Creator, and a reaffirmation of one's place within the interconnected web of life. This wisdom teaches us to see each day not as an isolated unit of time but as part of a greater rhythm that binds us to creation, community, and the divine.

Desert spirituality echoes these insights, emphasizing the need for intentional pauses. Early desert monastics would begin their day with silence and prayer, grounding themselves in God's presence before facing the challenges ahead. These practices are a reminder that beginning the day with devotion is not about escaping life's difficulties but about entering them with renewed strength and clarity.

Living the Daily Sabbath as Resistance

Practicing a devotional life is an act of resistance in a world that constantly interrupts with its demands, distractions, and pressures. It is a deliberate choice to interrupt the interruptions of urban, metropolitan, and anxious lives. For the urban commuter, life often feels like an endless cycle of discontinuity and high demands—rushing from one task to another, navigating crowded spaces, and contending with the relentless noise of modernity. In this environment, it can be difficult to situate oneself, to feel grounded or intentional amidst the chaos.

A daily Sabbath devotional creates sacred pauses in this churn, like making holes or cracking oppressive systems that seek to conform us into persons without will or intention. These systems—rooted in productivity, efficiency, and consumerism—pressure us to become mere cogs in a machine, driven by external demands rather than inner purpose. When we pause to reflect, pray, and meditate, we reclaim our autonomy, reminding ourselves and the world that we are not defined by what we produce or consume, but by who we are in God.

This act of resistance aligns with Abraham Heschel's understanding of the Sabbath as a "sanctuary in time."[38] Just as the Sabbath interrupts the weekly grind, a daily devotional interrupts the rapid pace of the urban commute and the constant pull of digital and material distractions. It is a way of saying, *I am not bound to this chaos; I belong to God.* By intentionally carving out time to connect with the divine, we disrupt the narratives that define our worth by our busyness or achievements.

For the urban commuter, this might mean reclaiming moments during transit—whether it's a few minutes of silent prayer on a crowded train, meditative reflection while waiting in traffic, or journaling in the quiet moments before the day begins. These devotional practices transform ordinary spaces into sacred ones, asserting that even in the midst of noise and rush, God's presence can be found, and peace can be cultivated.

Sabbath devotional living is not escapism; it is co-creation. It empowers us to engage the demands of life with intention and resilience. It reminds us that we are not slaves to the system but co-creators with God, invited to shape each day with hope and purpose. By grounding ourselves in God's presence daily, we become participants in divine rhythms that liberate rather than oppress.

Centering Thought

Let us embrace this daily Sabbath as a way of reclaiming time, renewing our spirit, and resisting the forces that would dehumanize us. By starting the day with a sacred pause, we not only center ourselves but also create space for the transformative work of God in our lives and the world.

Prayer

Jesus, make me like you!
Make me a person who begins each day with sacred intention,
open to your grace, guided by your word,
and co-creating a day filled with hope and purpose.

DEVOTIONAL LIFE

Personal Journal Prompts

- What sets the tone for your day when you wake up? Where is God's Spirit in that moment?
- Do you have a habit of journaling or reflecting on your daily thoughts and discoveries? How might this deepen your sense of connection with God and resist the forces conforming you into roles expected of you?
- What changes can you make in your daily routine to begin your day with God's presence and guidance?

Day 26

Righteous Compassion

Scripture

Don't judge, so that you won't be judged. You'll receive the same judgment you give. Whatever you deal out will be dealt out to you. . . . You deceive yourself! First take the log out of your eye, and then you'll see clearly to take the splinter out of your brother's or sister's eye.

—MATTHEW 7:1–2, 5 CEB

Embracing Compassion

NO ONE CAN TRULY be happy without compassion. While we recognize its importance, many of us still live within a culture of judgment and condemnation instead of fostering mutual respect and compassion. This tension reveals a fundamental contradiction in how we live as God's creation. Judgmental attitudes, often rooted in fears and insecurities, blind us to the divine image present in our neighbors.

In many Christianized cultures, particularly in the West, this contradiction is most visible in the perpetuation of gender and sex discrimination under the guise of biblical authority. When we judge others based on their identity, we project a distorted image of God, one that fosters hostility rather than mutual care. This judgmental mindset has fractured communities, corroded relationships, and turned the church into an environment of exclusion rather than reconciliation.

We live in a world under the ongoing cry of the crucified Jesus: "Father, forgive them, for they know not what they do" (Luke 23:34 ESV). Yet, many of us fail to recognize how deeply judgment and condemnation shape our behaviors. From pews to politics, we practice condemnation while preaching love, failing to embody the compassion of Jesus.

Gender and Sex Discrimination as Distorted Christian Identity

One of the most glaring failures of Christian practice across history has been its embrace of discrimination, particularly regarding gender and sexual identity, as a form of religious expression. This practice reflects a distorted understanding of holiness and Christian identity.

God's call to holiness is a call to *compassionate righteousness*, not a weapon of exclusion. Judgment, when devoid of compassion, dehumanizes others and undermines our shared humanity. Jesus calls us to love and maturity, recognizing that we are all bound by the same need for grace and redemption. This requires us to see others, not as enemies or competitors but as partners in the journey toward God's kingdom.

A False Image of God and Humanity

Jesus came to transform judgment and condemnation into compassion, reconciliation, and true righteousness. To condemn others without compassion is to reject Jesus, who embodied forgiveness even in the face of rejection and suffering. Compassion does not mean ignoring harmful behaviors but acknowledging that we all fall short and need redemption. It requires us to seek healing and reconciliation, seeing Christ in every person and every relationship.

Compassion begins with humility, recognizing that we do not know enough to judge others fully. It is a posture of repentance, a commitment to change, and an openness to grace. In practicing compassion, we reflect the love of Christ, whose righteousness was demonstrated through mercy, not condemnation.

The Colonial Algorithm as the Source of Condemnation

Much of our judgment stems from what can be described as a "colonial algorithm,"[39] a false hierarchy of humanity defined by rigid classifications—fourteen to be exact—such as *male, white, North Atlantic, learned, cisgender, married, fertile, Western Christian, conservative, capitalist, able (physically, mentally, emotionally, socioculturally), adult, productive, documented*. This algorithm dictates who is seen as worthy and who is marginalized, perpetuating systems of exclusion and oppression.

This false image of humanity codifies discrimination and reduces individuals to categories of worthiness based on social, cultural, and economic standards. It distorts the gospel and prioritizes human-made hierarchies over God's inclusive love.

Jesus Christ challenges us to dismantle this algorithm and embrace a vision of humanity rooted in the divine image. By recognizing God's presence in every person, we disrupt the structures that perpetuate judgment and condemnation. We are called to embody Christ's love by living as agents of reconciliation and justice.

Living Righteous Compassion

Practicing righteous compassion requires a willingness to engage with the pain of others without judgment, but with constructive tension. It is an act of faith that recognizes our shared humanity and dependence on God's grace. By rejecting the colonial algorithm and embracing Christ's example, we create communities that reflect God's kingdom—places of healing, inclusion, and hope.

Jesus teaches us that compassion is the antidote to judgment. It transforms relationships, restores dignity, and brings us closer to God's vision for humanity. To live with righteous compassion is to live in alignment with the heart of Christ, embodying the redemptive power of grace in a divided world.

Centering Thought

To live with righteous compassion is to embody the redemptive love of Jesus Christ in a world fractured by judgment, exclusion, and fear. It is a call to reject the false hierarchies of worth imposed by societal and cultural systems, embracing instead the truth that every person bears the image of God. By practicing compassion, we interrupt cycles of harm and create spaces where dignity, grace, and hope can flourish, becoming witnesses to God's inclusive and healing love.

Prayer

Jesus, free me from the colonial algorithm of condemnation.
Jesus, make me like you!
Make me a person who practices righteous compassion.

Personal Journal Prompts

- Reflect on a time when you felt judged or condemned. How did it affect you, and how did you respond?
- How do you feel when confronted with the colonial algorithm and its classifications of worthiness? Which classifications do you check?

- Have you ever expressed judgment based on gender, race, or other discriminatory factors? What steps can you take to overcome these biases?
- What actions or attitudes of compassion can you cultivate in your life to reflect Jesus's teachings more fully?

Day 27

Stumbling in Perseverance

Scripture

This one thing I do: forgetting what lies behind and straining forward to what lies ahead, I press on toward the goal for the prize of the heavenly call of God in Christ Jesus.

—PHILIPPIANS 3:13–14

Embracing Stumbles in Perseverance

TO LIVE IS TO stumble, and to stumble is a sign that we are alive. While this may initially seem pessimistic, it is, in fact, a profound truth that underscores the vitality of human existence. Jesus himself acknowledged this reality when he prepared his disciples for the trials ahead, saying: "I have said these things to you to keep you from falling away [stumbling] . . . so that in me you may have peace. In the world, you face persecution, but take courage: I have conquered the world!" (John 16:1, 33). Recognizing this truth has always been vital for those seeking to follow Christ faithfully.

How Ancients and Moderns Approach Existential Threats

Ancient civilizations understood stumbling as part of a communal journey, often seeking meaning and resilience through shared narratives, religious rituals, and philosophical frameworks. Whether in the myths of the Aztecs, the philosophical teachings of Confucianism, or the communal resilience of African tribal communities, stumbling was seen as a collective challenge to overcome together.

In contrast, the modern metropolitan individual often faces stumbling blocks in isolation. Urban life exacerbates this fragmentation, with its high demands and relentless pace, leaving little room for communal narratives of perseverance. The focus on individualism, material success, and rapid technological advancement often magnifies feelings of inadequacy and despair when obstacles arise. Consequently, many modern individuals lack the communal support and spiritual frameworks necessary to recover from life's inevitable disruptions.

Christian Spirituality and Perseverance

In Christian spirituality, perseverance is the primary muscle of obedience. It is the disposition to continuing faithfully after stumbling, ensuring that our journey retains its momentum despite interruptions. The image of Jesus falling on the *Via Dolorosa* has shaped Christian discipleship since the early days of the church. The history of Christianity itself reflects this reality: while the church as an institution has often stumbled, the body of Christ perseveres through repentance, confession, and obedience to the Spirit.

The persevering Christian embarks on life with a clear vision of God's priorities, fully aware of the stumbling blocks ahead. They do not deny the difficulties but trust in God's presence through every trial. They echo the psalmist's words: "Even though I walk through the darkest valley, I fear no evil; for you are with me; your rod and your staff—they comfort me" (Ps 23:4). In Jesus Christ, we find the ultimate model of perseverance: his unwavering obedience to the cross demonstrates how to press on despite fear, pain, and opposition.

Living with Stumbles and Anxiety

Stumbling can often trigger anxiety, creating a mental block that amplifies fears of failure. Anxiety hinders our ability to recover, leading to cycles of self-doubt and hesitation. Yet, in Jesus Christ, we find the strength to transform anxiety into renewal energy. Through faith and reliance on the Holy Spirit, moments of stumbling become opportunities for growth, resilience, and deeper dependence on God. Jesus teaches us that stumbling is not the end but part of the journey toward a fuller life in him.

Centering Thought

Stumbling is not failure but a profound reminder of our humanity and our need for God. In Jesus Christ, stumbling becomes a sacred opportunity—a place where perseverance is forged, anxiety is transformed into renewed energy, and faith grows deeper. In every stumble, we are invited to rely, not on our own strength but on the Spirit of God who equips us to persevere and transform challenges into steps of growth, resilience, and divine purpose.

Prayer

Jesus, make me like you!
Make me a persevering person,
a resilient disciple able to turn anxiety into renewal energy,
by the power of the Spirit.

Personal Journal Prompts

- Reflect on a time when you encountered a stumbling block. What was your initial response, and how did you handle it?
- Is it difficult for you to recover and carry on after stumbling? How does anxiety play a role in this struggle?
- What place does Jesus have in your decisions, priorities, and commitments? How can you allow his example of perseverance to guide you through your stumbles?

Day 28

Obedient Leadership

Scripture

If I, your Lord and Teacher, have washed your feet, you too must wash each other's feet. I have given you an example: Just as I have done, you also must do. . . . Since you know these things, you will be happy if you do them.

—John 13:14–15, 17

Understanding Obedient Leadership

The essence of Christian leadership is service (Mark 10:42–45). No one can experience true joy without serving others. Genuine service arises from inner abundance, creative love, and irresistible grace, transforming into obedient leadership. Service is not limited to personal acts of kindness but is deeply political. It shapes how we navigate systems of power, relationships, and shared responsibilities in the world.

Service, however, is often tainted by ulterior motives. Some serve only those they love, others serve to gain favors, and some serve solely out of fear of losing privilege. At times, even within

Christian contexts, service becomes transactional—a game of influence and benefit. This false service distorts the call to lead in humility and love.

True Christian service, or Christopraxis, transforms convenient leadership into an act of radical obedience to God, not a strategy for self-advancement. It calls us to serve our neighbors, not out of convenience but out of conviction, motivated by God's love and grace.

The Source of Obedient Leadership

Obedient leadership begins with the conviction that service is an essential aspect of God's kingdom. It is not rooted in influence, outcomes, or recognition but in love for God and neighbor. Service in the Christian life fulfills God's law of love and reflects the self-giving nature of Christ.

In Jesus Christ, we see the ultimate servant leader who washed the feet of his disciples and demonstrated that leadership is about empowering others, not asserting dominance. His obedience to God's will, even to the point of death, models the humility and perseverance required to serve faithfully.

Through the Holy Spirit, we are empowered to live out this obedience in our own lives, prioritizing relationships over results and aligning our actions with God's redemptive purposes in the world. This leadership is not about asserting authority but about cultivating mutual care, sacrifice, and shared responsibility in our communities.

Jesus: The Palestinian, Jewish Servant of Creation

Jesus Christ, a Palestinian Jew, embodies the servant of creation *par excellence*. He demonstrated the transformative power of humble service, breaking down barriers of race, class, and gender. His leadership was rooted in love, sacrifice, and joy, calling his followers to "wash one another's feet" (John 13:14) as a sign of mutual care and solidarity.

True servant leadership, inspired by Christ, does not seek greatness but achieves it through acts of humility and grace. It is a quiet, yet powerful, expression of God's love, challenging the hierarchies and systems that perpetuate oppression. As Martin Luther King Jr. reminded us, "We can all be great because we can all serve."

Leading by Obeying: Lessons from the Indigenous Zapatista Movement

A profound example of servant leadership that resonates with Jesus's Christopraxis is found in the Indigenous Zapatista philosophy of leadership: ruling by obeying the community. This approach, rooted in Indigenous wisdom, prioritizes collective well-being and ensures that leaders remain accountable to the people they serve.

The Indigenous Zapatista model rejects authoritarianism and hierarchical power, emphasizing shared decision-making and mutual respect. Leaders are not above the community but part of it, entrusted with the responsibility to listen, learn, and act in alignment with the collective needs and aspirations of the people. This reflects the servant leadership of Jesus, who did not come to be served but to serve and to give his life for others.

Incorporating this model into Christian leadership challenges the church to move away from individualism and clericalism toward a communal and participatory practice of ministry. It calls us to prioritize the voices of the marginalized, honor the dignity of all, and work collaboratively to advance God's kingdom on earth.

The Indigenous Zapatista principle of *leading by obeying* aligns with Jesus's teaching that greatness is found in serving others. It offers a countercultural vision of leadership that resists domination, centers the community, and fosters an environment of mutual care and shared purpose. By adopting this approach, Christian leaders can embody the redemptive power of God's love and create spaces where justice, compassion, and hope flourish.

Centering Thought

Servant leadership, modeled by Jesus of Nazareth, calls us to a life of humble obedience and mutual empowerment. It challenges the hierarchical norms of power by embracing the wisdom of communities and embodying love, justice, and service. In *leading by obeying*, we align ourselves with God's call to foster collective flourishing, dismantle oppression, and create spaces where all voices are valued, reflecting the inclusive and liberating reign of Christ.

Prayer

*Jesus, free me from false service
and make me like you!
Make me a servant leader who rules by obeying,
moved by love and grace.*

Personal Journal Prompts

- Reflect on your experiences with leadership. How do you balance serving others out of convenience with leading them out of obedience?
- What does *leading by obeying* mean to you? How can it transform your approach to leadership?
- How can the principles of servant leadership, as modeled by Jesus and embodied in the Zapatista movement, help you address pressing challenges like systemic injustice, economic disparity, and political oppression?
- In what ways can you practice obedient leadership in your daily life, fostering community and mutual care?

Day 29

Intimacy with God
Believing *Where* We Are

Scripture

*The Spirit searches all things, even the deep things of God.
For who knows a person's thoughts except their own spirit within them?
In the same way no one knows the thoughts
of God except the Spirit of God.
What we have received is not the spirit of the world,
but the Spirit who is from God,
so that we may understand what God has freely given us.*

—1 Corinthians 2:10–12 NIV

The Depths of Divine Intimacy

ONLY THOSE WHO DARE to deepen their relationship with God experience true intimacy and joy. Superficiality is the boundary that limits all relationships. When we meet someone for the first time, we decide whether to remain on the surface or to explore the depths of a relationship, risking vulnerability to cultivate intimacy. Superficial relationships keep us distant, without risk or personal investment. While they may seem easier, they lack reciprocity, affection, and true empathy. Living on the surface is akin to sailing endlessly across an ocean without diving into its waters, never witnessing the beauty and mystery of the world beneath.

God, however, is a being of depths and mysteries. We can only know God if God chooses to reveal God's self to us, crossing the boundary of the divine depths into our superficial realm to invite us back into God's sacred mystery. God has always taken the initiative, meeting us at the surface where many of us prefer to stay—safe, uncommitted, and without demands. But once God self-reveals and draws us in with divine love, God invites us to the depths of intimacy. This divine intimacy is a transformative journey of belonging, marked by unconditional surrender, mutual affection, sacrificial love, and the discovery of God's character and intentions. It is the difference between merely knowing *about* God and truly *knowing* God.

Paradoxically, truly knowing God results in truly knowing ourselves—individually, collectively, and cosmically. It is an intersectional epistemology (way of knowing). This intersectional, theological epistemology prepares us to truly fulfill the greatest biblical commandments: "'Love the Lord your God with all your heart and with all your soul and with all your mind.' This is the first and greatest commandment. And the second is like it: 'Love your neighbor as yourself'" (Matt 22:37–39 NIV).

God's Invitation into the Depths

The Eastern Christian spiritual tradition, particularly in hesychasm, speaks of this journey into intimacy as a movement from external distractions to internal stillness where God dwells. This "prayer of the heart," as taught by the desert fathers and mothers, mirrors God's initiative in drawing us into the divine mystery. By quieting the noise of the surface world and listening for the Spirit within, we cultivate a relationship that transforms both our inner life and how we engage the outer world.

Similarly, Indigenous spiritualities emphasize relational depth with the divine through creation. The land, its rhythms, and its sacredness provide a pathway to intimacy with the Creator. By attuning ourselves to the cycles of nature and living in harmony with creation, we practice a spirituality of interconnectedness, where divine intimacy is experienced, not apart from life but woven into it.

World religions also echo this pursuit of divine depth. In Hinduism, the concept of *bhakti* (devotion) involves cultivating an intimate, loving relationship with the divine through surrender and trust. In Islam, the practice of *dhikr* (remembrance) calls believers to continually seek God's presence in every moment. In Buddhism, the meditative journey of mindfulness invites practitioners to strip away illusions and encounter ultimate reality *where we are*.

The Bridge to Divine Intimacy and Augustine of Hippo

Jesus Christ, in Augustine's theology, represents the incarnational movement of God entering the human condition, descending into the realm of our temporal and "fallen" existence to reconcile us to divine truth and love.[40] The phrase "in Christ" conveys, for Augustine, our participation in God's being, emphasizing the transformative union with God made possible through Christ's redemptive work and the sacraments.

Through the Holy Spirit, the love of God is poured into our hearts (cf. Romans 5:5), drawing us into the intimate relationship of the Trinity. The Spirit functions as the divine bond uniting believers with Christ, and through him, with the Father, leading us into deeper communion. This process is not merely about entering a throne room of grace but about being incorporated into the eternal love of the Trinity as adopted children (Lat. *adoptio filiorum Dei*), fully participating in the goodness and life of God.[41]

At Christ's baptism, we see this intimacy on full display: "You are my Son, the Beloved; with you I am well pleased" (Luke 3:22). In Christ, we receive the same baptism of love, marking us as God's beloved. This is the heart of divine intimacy—living moment by moment desiring God's presence and seeking it in God's word, in our own being, in our neighbors, and in creation.

Living God's Intimacy as Resistance

In today's urban, fast-paced existence, intimacy with God becomes an act of resistance against superficiality, performativity, and disconnection. Modern life often prioritizes efficiency, productivity, and external validation, leaving little room for cultivating deep relationships with others or with God. Practicing intimacy with God interrupts this cycle. It invites us to pause, to listen, to reorient ourselves, and to dwell in the presence of the Divine amid the chaos of daily life. We will always be authentic because we are *where* we believe, namely, participating in God's incarnated ecology of love and justice (*Summun Bonum*).

Desert spirituality reminds us that intimacy is cultivated, not in comfort but in solitude, struggle, and surrender to community. The desert, both literal and metaphorical, strips away distractions and reveals our dependence on God. It teaches us that intimacy requires vulnerability, and vulnerability requires trust—a trust that God's love is unshakable and ever-present.

Centering Thought

To seek intimacy with God is to embrace the courage to leave the safety of the surface and dive into the depths of divine mystery. Through Christ's Spirit, we are invited into a relationship of trust, love, and surrender, where we discover God's presence, not only in sacred moments but also in the fabric of daily life. As we embrace this intimacy, we resist the superficiality of modern existence, cultivating a life rooted in vulnerability, stillness, reorientation, and profound connection with God, creation, and one another. Let the depths of God's love shape your being, drawing you into the fullness of divine belonging and purpose, wherever we live.

Prayer

Jesus, make me like you!
Draw me into your depths.
Make me a person of divine intimacy,
eager to explore the mystery of your love,
and to find you in myself, my neighbor, and creation.

Personal Journal Prompts

- Do you tend to prefer superficial or deep relationships? Why?
- What risks have you taken in your journey toward intimacy with others or with God?
- What prevents you from cultivating a deeper relationship with God? And with others?
- What do you think sharing your faith will look like through superficial relationships?

Day 30

Trust

Scripture

Wounds from a friend can be trusted, but an enemy multiplies kisses.
—Proverbs 27:6 NIV

My sheep hear my voice. I know them, and they follow me.
—John 10:27 NIV

—[Love] bears all things, believes all things, hopes all things, endures all things.
—1 Corinthians 13:7

The Necessity of Trust

TRUST IS FUNDAMENTAL TO human flourishing. Without trust, relationships, communities, and systems crumble, leaving us isolated and purposeless. Trust allows us to build families, nurture friendships, sustain faith, and engage meaningfully with others.

Conversely, distrust fractures these bonds, leading to isolation and despair, pushing us toward a self-centered and alienated existence.

The ambiguity of human nature complicates our relationship with trust. On the one hand, people often fail to meet our expectations, leading to hurt and betrayal. On the other, a worldview steeped in cynicism—believing no one is trustworthy—results in further alienation. Behavioral psychology teaches us that trust is built through consistent, transparent actions over time. Yet breaches of trust, whether in personal relationships or toxic ministry settings, often result in emotional wounds, defensiveness, and even burnout, perpetuating cycles of mistrust and harm.

God's Trust in Humanity

Despite humanity's ambiguity, God extends divine trust toward us. This trust is not naïve but rooted in grace and a willingness to engage relationally with human frailty. Rather than overpowering human freedom, God covenants with us, embodying patience and presence through the Holy Spirit.

The Spirit works within us, transforming us from unreliable and self-centered individuals into trustworthy disciples (Acts 2:37). Through this relationship, God invites us into a co-creative partnership, cultivating faithfulness, reliability, and mutual trust. Divine trust, therefore, is not a transactional expectation but a transformational process that inspires us to live with integrity.

Trust Restored in Christ

Trust finds its ultimate ground in Jesus Christ. Jesus, as the embodiment of divine faithfulness, redeems our brokenness and teaches us to live as trustworthy people. Through his life, death, and resurrection, he inaugurates a reign founded on trust, love, justice, and peace.

Jesus's relationships were marked by forgiveness and restoration (Luke 4). His trust in Peter after his denial and his compassionate engagement with the doubting Thomas are testaments to his transformative leadership. As followers of Christ, we are called to emulate this trustworthiness in our relationships, embodying grace and reconciliation.

The church, as the Body of Christ, is tasked with being a community of trust, a grounding community of the Spirit, in a culture of suspicion and division. Through humility, mutual care, and faithful witness, we become agents of trustworthiness, reflecting the reliability of Christ in our fractured world. Are unchurched populations perceiving Christian churches as communities of trust? This is not an easy question for Christian churches in our time.

Living Together Interculturally in a Christian Culture of Distrust

In many Christian contexts, particularly in the United States, a culture of distrust has taken root. This manifests as "othering" based on doctrinal differences, political affiliations, migration status, or identities such as Muslim, Jewish, or queer. Instead of embodying Jesus's radical hospitality, Christian doctrine and Scripture are often weaponized to alienate and exclude.

However, Matt 25:31–46 reminds us that Jesus, the living Word of God, identifies with the marginalized and dispossessed. He challenges us to encounter him in the stranger, the undocumented, and the unproductive—those often deemed "least" by society. Recognizing Christ in the "other" disrupts capitalist, colonial, and hyper-individualistic metrics of worth, calling us instead to embrace the divine image in all people. But how do we do it?

Reimagining Intercultural Community in Christ

1. Seeing Christ in the Other

Following Jesus means recognizing his presence in those we find difficult to welcome. By cultivating humility and curiosity, we can dismantle biases and prejudices that prevent genuine connection.

The question is not whether Jesus is present in the other, but whether we have eyes to see him there.

2. A Decolonial Approach to Community

Christian interculturality requires learning from those marginalized by systems of oppression. Instead of forcing assimilation or imposing cultural norms, we are called to create spaces where diverse expressions of faith and life flourish. Indigenous spiritualities, for example, offer profound insights into interconnectedness and stewardship, enriching our understanding of God's reign.

3. Practicing Prophetic Imagination

Drawing on prophetic imagination, we can critique exclusionary narratives and envision a countercultural reality of inclusion and peace. This involves:

- Advocating for the dignity and rights of religious and cultural minorities.
- Fostering welcoming communities for migrants, queer individuals, and those excluded by societal norms.
- Reimagining church structures to prioritize relationality and mutuality over hierarchy and control.

Toward a Constructive Vision of Christian Interculturality

Living as a trustworthy Christian community requires deep engagement, solidarity, and shared life across differences. As the Zapatista dictum suggests, we must cultivate "a world where many worlds fit," reflecting the diverse unity of God's unfolding kingdom. This vision calls for:

- Listening deeply to marginalized voices.

- Breaking barriers of mistrust through humility and learning.
- Celebrating diverse expressions of faith and culture that mirror God's image in humanity.
- Embodying Jesus's radical hospitality and justice and becoming a sanctuary of trustworthiness, a grounding community of the Spirit, that bridges divides and extends God's love to a world in need.

Centering Thought

Trust is the foundation of Christian community and intercultural living. By seeing Christ in the marginalized and dismantling barriers of distrust, we embody the gospel's call to radical love and hospitality.

Prayer

Jesus, make me like you!
Help me see you in those who challenge my comfort.
Transform me into a trustworthy disciple, a builder of trust,
and a vessel of your reconciling love.

Personal Journal Prompts

- When have you struggled to trust others or felt distrusted yourself? How did this affect you?
- How can you identify and dismantle biases that prevent you from seeing Jesus Christ in the "other"?
- What steps can you take to build trust in your community, workplace, or church?
- How does Jesus's life inspire you to become a trustworthy and trusting disciple?

Day 31

Comfort

Scripture

The Lord will sustain them on their sickbed;
in their illness you heal all their infirmities.

—Psalm 41:3

It is to your advantage that I go away; for if I don't go away, the comforting Counselor will not come to you. However, if I do go, I will send him to you.

—John 16:7 CJB

The Necessity of Comfort

LIFE IS FULL OF challenges, and no one can find true happiness without the balm of comfort. When we endure crises without receiving comfort, emotional scars form within us, often resurfacing as sadness or bitterness. Unaddressed grief leaves a void, reflecting loneliness, misunderstanding, and a lack of love.

Although we may deny it, everyone needs comfort. At times, we reject the consoling efforts of others during our struggles, yet inwardly we long for a tender, healing presence. This paradox reveals our human vulnerability—while outwardly pushing others away, we inwardly desire the soothing touch of compassion. It is painful when those around us fail to understand this ambiguity, leaving us feeling even more isolated.

Comfort, at its core, is a gentle caress of the heart. It is an act of presence that speaks to the heart's deep need for reassurance, healing, and connection.

God as the Ultimate Comforter

One of the most profound images of God in Scripture is that of a shepherd tenderly caring for their flock. The shepherd's task includes tending to the wounded sheep, providing solace and care. As the psalmist declares, "Your rod and your staff—they comfort me" (Ps 23:4).

In the New Testament, God self-reveals in an even more intimate role: as the Comforter, the Holy Spirit. This revelation underscores God's nature as a healer of the brokenhearted and a companion to the weary. Comfort is not merely about solving problems but about being a healing presence that restores and renews.

Jesus Christ, the Good Shepherd, did not abandon us when he ascended to the Father. Instead, he and his Father sent the Spirit of the Resurrected One to dwell within us as the ultimate source of comfort. No sorrow or pain is too great for the Spirit who raised the "man of sorrows and acquainted with infirmity" (Isa 53:3) from the tomb. Through the Spirit, we are united to Jesus Christ in an unbreakable bond of healing and hope.

Learning to Comfort Through Christ, the Wounded Healer

Jesus came to heal the brokenhearted (Isa 61:1; Luke 4:18), and in him we find the model for comforting others. His ministry was marked by acts of compassion, whether gently restoring dignity to the outcast, mourning with the grieving, or extending grace to the downtrodden. His presence itself was a source of comfort, reminding those he encountered that they were seen, loved, and valued by God.

As followers of Jesus Christ, we are called to emulate his comforting presence. The church, as the body of Christ, is a wounded community of healing and consolation—a sanctuary for the broken and weary. In a world that often isolates and neglects the vulnerable, the church must stand as a community of the Spirit, offering comfort and care to those in need.

The Psychology of Comfort

From a psychological perspective, comfort is deeply tied to human connection and the regulation of emotions. Emotional validation, active listening, and empathetic presence are crucial in fostering healing. Comfort is not about fixing someone's pain but about standing with them in their suffering, offering solidarity and hope.

When comfort is withheld, it can lead to emotional withdrawal, resentment, or even despair. Conversely, providing comfort fosters resilience, rebuilding trust and a sense of belonging. Learning to give and receive comfort is an essential aspect of emotional and spiritual maturity.

Embracing Comfort in a World of Pain

Comfort challenges the pervasive culture of distrust and alienation, a source of pain in our world. In a society where strength is often equated with self-reliance, admitting our need for comfort can feel like a weakness. Yet, in truth, it is an act of courage to seek solace and to offer it to others.

Drawing on Indigenous spiritualities and Eastern Christian traditions, comfort is understood, not merely as a personal experience but as a communal practice. The sacred act of being present with someone in their pain—whether through a shared silence, a prayer, or a ritual of care—reflects the interconnectedness of all life. These traditions teach us that comfort is not about removing suffering but about creating a sacred space where healing and renewal can take place.

Living as a Community of Comfort

To be a community of comfort is to live as Christ's community of healing in the world, embodying his love for the brokenhearted. This requires us to cultivate practices of deep listening, empathy, and mutual care. In the words of Henri Nouwen, we are called to be "wounded healers"—offering the comfort we have received to others.[42]

Comfort, as an act of faith, reminds us that we are never alone. The Spirit dwells within us, and heals through us, uniting us to Christ, one another, and creation. Together, we can bear the burdens of life, finding strength in the compassionate presence of God and his people.

Centering Thought

Comfort is a caress of the whole person, a reminder that we are not alone in our struggles. In Jesus Christ, we are called to receive and offer the healing presence of God, becoming a community of the Spirit who accompanies a world longing for solace.

Prayer

Jesus, make me like you!
Make me comforted in the power of the Spirit,
a person-in-community who consoles the brokenhearted,
a presence of healing and hope in the world.

COMFORT

Personal Journal Prompts

- Have you experienced a crisis without receiving comfort? How did it shape you?
- Do you find it easy or difficult to accept comfort? Why?
- How did Jesus console those around him? How did Jesus's disciples follow his conforming example in their context?
- Who in your community or circle needs your comforting presence today? How can you advocate against wounding structures victimizing the most vulnerable in your context?

Day 32

Sensuous Reason (*Sentipensar*)

Scripture

Truly I tell you, unless you change and become like little children, you will never enter the kingdom of heaven.

—MATTHEW 18:3 NIV

Embracing the Depth of Feeling and Sensing

WE CANNOT FULLY LIVE without sensing and feeling. Through our God-given capacity for sensuous reasoning, we find meaning, appreciate beauty, and form connections—or sometimes reject what we experience. Denying this dimension of our humanity, as rationalism often does, severs a vital part of who we are. Similarly, exalting feelings and emotions above all other aspects of life leads to sensationalism, which distorts the balance necessary for true flourishing.

To live sensuously (*orthopathos*) is to honor our capacity to perceive God, others, and creation inwardly. It allows us to connect deeply without distorting or forcing others into false images of themselves. This holistic engagement applies to our relationships with one another, with God, and with Mother Earth.

Sensing is a language of the reflective heart—a spiritual organ of perception that enables us to move beyond words into the sacred rhythms of life. As children, we instinctively live in this sensuous state, embracing imagination and emotion. However, as we grow, societal pressures often teach us to mistrust and suppress this capacity instead of refining it. By doing so, we lose sensitivity to the mystery and beauty of the world around us.

Indigenous Wisdom and *Sentipensar*

Mesoamerican Indigenous traditions offer profound insights into the interplay of feeling and thinking, often captured in the concept of *sentipensar*—a harmonious blend of sensing and reasoning. This holistic wisdom recognizes that emotions and intellect are not opposing forces but complementary tools for understanding life and navigating relationships.

Practicing *sentipensar* invites us to approach the world with a sense of wonder and connection. It aligns with the teachings of Jesus, who calls us to live with childlike sensitivity to God's presence and creation. By integrating our capacity to feel and think, we can engage more deeply with others, cultivate humility, and foster healing in a fragmented world. This practice transforms relationships, deepens spirituality, and broadens our ecological awareness.

Jesus Christ: The Revealer of Spiritual Senses

Jesus Christ came to reveal the depths of God's love and teach us to perceive the divine through spiritual senses (Heb 5:14). In calling us to become like children, Jesus invites us to reclaim our capacity for wonder, trust, and emotional honesty. In him, we are trained to sense the Spirit's rhythms and discern God's presence in every aspect of life, from the grand movements of the cosmos to the quiet stirrings of the heart.

Through Christ, we learn to care for creation with humility. Recognizing the sacredness of the natural world—a gift from God, not a resource to exploit—is an act of worship. Scripture abounds with ecological imagery: the tree of life, rivers of healing, and the promise of a new heaven and new earth. To sense God is to honor creation as a reflection of divine love and to serve as its stewards.

Jesus's life embodies this ecological humility. By emptying himself to become fully human (Phil 2:7), Jesus demonstrated the ultimate act of service to God and creation. This self-emptying love challenges us to reject exploitative attitudes and embrace a posture of care and reverence for the earth and all its inhabitants.

Living as Companions in Ecological Healing

To live sensuously in Christ is to participate in the Spirit's work of healing and renewal. This requires an attitude of *ecological humility*, recognizing that humanity is not the pinnacle of creation but a part of a greater whole. Seeing creation as a living, sacred gift calls us to serve it with the same obedience and love that Christ modeled.

In embracing this perspective, we dismantle the hierarchies and dominion narratives that have distorted our relationship with the earth. Instead, we cultivate an ethic of stewardship, grounded in the interconnectedness of all life. Those who truly sense the Spirit in each moment live, not with pride or dominance but with a deep sense of responsibility and reverence.

Centering Thought

To sense God is to embrace the sacred rhythms of life, perceiving his presence in creation, relationships, and every present moment. In Jesus Christ, we learn to harmonize our feelings and thoughts, becoming companions in the Spirit's work of healing and renewal.

Sensuous Reason (Sentipensar)

Prayer

Jesus, make me like you!
Transform my domineering into ecological service.
Someone who senses God in everything and every present moment.

Personal Journal Prompts

- Reflect on what it means to feel God's presence. How does this experience shape your faith and your relationships with others?
- Consider your reactions to others' emotions. How do you respond to expressions of joy, sorrow, or anger? What do these reactions reveal about your own emotional and relational patterns?
- Recall a time when you felt deeply connected to God or creation. How did this experience change your perspective or actions toward the world?
- What steps can you take to embody ecological humility and service, participating in the healing of creation through your attitudes and actions?

Day 33

Obsession
A Holy Fixation on God's Liberative Love

Scripture

For the message about the cross is foolishness
to those who are perishing,
but to us who are being saved it is the power of God.

—1 Corinthians 1:18

He died for all, so that those who live might
live no longer for themselves,
but for Him who died and was raised for them.

—2 Corinthians 5:15

Breaking the Chains of Obsession

AT SOME POINT IN life, we all grapple with obsessive thoughts—those relentless ideas that consume our minds and direct our actions. When we fail to break free from their grip, we become puppets, slaves to our obsessions, unable to live in peace. Overcoming such obsessions requires cultivating a new kind of persistent thought, one that liberates us, restores serenity, and anchors our lives in meaningful purpose.

In the Christian tradition, transformation occurs when the mind undergoes death and resurrection in Christ—a process known as repentance (*metanoia*). To be free, we must allow harmful obsessions to die so that we may be reborn into a new, liberating obsession: Jesus Christ. This is not mere thought replacement but a spiritual reorientation of our entire being, centered on the life, death, and resurrection of Jesus Christ, our contemporary, as Bonhoeffer would say.[43]

The "Foolish" Obsession of Early Christians

In the early centuries of the church, the Christian faith was often viewed as irrational, even mad. Who, after all, would willingly suffer persecution and death for the sake of a failure, that is, crucified leader—a man executed as a criminal under Roman law? Yet, to the early Christians, this so-called "madness" was the ultimate wisdom and power of God (1 Cor 1:21–23).

For example, the martyrdom of Polycarp, a second-century bishop of Smyrna, exemplifies this transformative obsession. Arrested and brought before Roman authorities, he was offered his life if he would only renounce Christ. Polycarp's response remains iconic: "Eighty-six years I have served Him, and He has done me no wrong. How can I blaspheme my King who saved me?"[44]

His unshakable fixation on Christ, even in the face of death, demonstrated a liberated mind consumed, not by fear but by faith. For these early believers, the resurrection of Christ was the new obsession that redefined their identity, relationships, and purpose. They no longer lived for themselves but for him who died and rose again. This shift did not lead to enslavement but to freedom—freedom to live fully, love boldly, and endure with hope. How I wish I could say the same about us, modern metropolitan Christians!

Jesus Christ: The Liberating Obsession

Jesus Christ is the one liberating *obsession* capable of granting true freedom and peace. In him, we find a life unshackled from the tyranny of pleasure, domination, or fear. Those who lose everything for the sake of Jesus Christ discover their true selves, their ultimate value, a reconciled community, and a glorious destiny.

This liberation is not abstract; it is embodied in daily life. To follow Christ is to take up our cross, not as a burden of despair but as an act of profound sensibility and purpose. It is to live with the resilience of resurrection and the power of the Spirit poured out at Pentecost.

Examples abound in history of those who embodied this obsession with Christ:

- **Fr. Bartolomé de Las Casas** who, driven by the compassionate justice of Jesus, stood against European genocidal colonialism in favor of the human rights of the Indigenous populations of the Americas.
- **Dietrich Bonhoeffer** who stood against Nazi tyranny, driven by his commitment to Christ and the call to resist evil.
- **Chiara Lubich,** founder of the Focolare Movement, who built communities of radical love and unity in a divided world.
- **Countless unnamed believers** who, in the face of suffering and loss, have clung to Christ, finding hope and strength to persevere.

Toward a Christ-Centered Mind

Obsession shapes behavior until it is replaced by another, stronger fixation. By fixing our minds on Jesus Christ (Heb 12), we cultivate a transformative obsession that brings peace and purpose. The apostle Paul urges us to "set your minds on things above" (Col 3:2 NIV), a call to align our thoughts with the will and wisdom of God.

In practical terms, this means:

- Meditating on Scripture (*such as Lectio Divina*) to renew our minds (Rom 12:2).
- Practicing gratitude in community to counter negative fixations.
- Engaging in prayer and worship to center our hearts on God.
- Committing to acts of service that reflect Christ's love and purpose in favor of the most vulnerable.

In Christ, obsessive thoughts rooted in phobias or self-centeredness are replaced with a holy fixation on God's liberative love. This shift is not immediate but requires daily surrender and practice—a continual process of dying to ourselves and rising in Christ.

Centering Thought

Jesus Christ is the liberating obsession who transforms our lives from enslavement to freedom. To live for him is to find peace, purpose, and a love that sustains us in every circumstance.

Prayer

Jesus, make me like you!
Transform my obsessions into a holy fixation on you.
A person liberated by your love and driven
to fulfill the will of the Father.

Personal Journal Prompts

- What obsessive thoughts have dominated your life, and how have they affected your relationships and well-being?
- How does the example of previous Christian martyrs inspire you to fix your mind on Christ's liberative love?

- What daily practices can help you focus on Jesus and his purposes for your life?
- How does living with a holy fixation on Christ transform your understanding of freedom and peace?

Day 34

Poor in Spirit

Scripture

Blessed are the poor in spirit, for theirs is the kingdom of heaven.

—Matthew 5:3

You say, "I am rich; I have prospered, and I need nothing." You do not realize that you are wretched, pitiable, poor, blind, and naked. Therefore, I counsel you to buy from me gold refined by fire so that you may be rich, and white robes to clothe you and to keep the shame of your nakedness from being seen, and salve to anoint your eyes so that you may see.

—Revelation 3:17–18

Embracing Poverty in Spirit

To GROW IN HUMILITY is to open the door to true happiness. Only those who have grown enough to embrace poverty in spirit can fully experience the riches of God's kingdom. Poverty in spirit encompasses two core virtues: humility and care for the destitute. Its opposite—spiritual pride—manifests as greed (root of exploitation).

The spiritually proud and greedy operate from a distorted conviction: *I am chosen, a child of the King, heir to all the glorious riches of the universe, spiritually privileged, and deserving of the best life can offer.* This mindset, often cloaked in Christian language of exceptionalism, is antithetical to the gospel and misrepresents the heart of Jesus Christ. Such spiritual pride leads us to see ourselves as superior, fostering an elitism that blinds us to the true nature of God's kingdom—a kingdom for the humble and the poor.

The prophetic warning in Revelation is a direct challenge to this mindset: "You say, 'I am rich' . . . but you do not realize that you are wretched, pitiable, poor, blind, and naked" (3:17 NIV). This is not just a critique of material wealth but a call to recognize our spiritual destitution without God. Only by acknowledging our deep need for grace can we truly embrace the humility and dependence required to live as citizens of God's kingdom.

The Ethics of the Kingdom

A dear colleague who is now with the Lord, Glenn Stassen, was holy obsessed with Jesus's ethics, and his book *Kingdom Ethics* offers a compelling framework for understanding this beatitude.[45] Stassen highlights that Jesus's call to poverty in spirit is not merely an individual virtue but a communal posture that embodies the values of God's upside-down kingdom—a kingdom where power is found in servanthood, wealth in generosity, and greatness in humility.

In Jesus's kingdom, the "poor in spirit" are those who:

- Recognize their dependence on God, refusing to see themselves as self-sufficient.
- Relinquish the pursuit of materialism, power, and status, focusing instead on serving others.
- Engage in radical care for the marginalized, ensuring that the weak, poor, and vulnerable are prioritized.

This ethic directly challenges modern Christian tendencies toward prosperity gospel and spiritual triumphalism. A gospel that equates divine favor with wealth, success, and influence betrays the message of Jesus of Nazareth, who chose to live as a servant, identifying with the lowly and the oppressed.

Jesus Christ: The Poor in Spirit

Jesus came to overcome the temptations of materialism, ministerial shortcuts, and the misuse of power. Though he was God, he emptied himself, taking the form of a servant (Phil 2:6–7). This act of self-emptying—*kenosis*—is the ultimate example of poverty in spirit.

Through his life and ministry, Jesus revealed that true spiritual richness comes from humility and care for the poor. He called his followers to embody this same humility, living as the poor of the kingdom who prioritize the needs of the world's poor.

To be poor in spirit is to live with the awareness that we (all) are unworthy yet receive everything from God. It is becoming the poor in spirit by following Jesus in living for the sake of the weak, the vulnerable, and the marginalized—those whom the world sees as last but whom God sees as first in the redemptive work of his kingdom.

Examples from church history illustrate this kingdom ethic in action:

- **St. Francis of Assisi** who renounced his wealth to live in solidarity with the poor, embodying Christ's humility and care for the destitute.

- **Dorothy Day,** founder of the Catholic Worker Movement, who dedicated her life to serving the homeless and advocating for social justice.

- **Desmond Tutu** who used his platform to amplify the voices of the oppressed during apartheid in South Africa, demonstrating that spiritual poverty demands action on behalf of the marginalized.

Living as the Poor in Spirit

To embrace poverty in spirit requires a daily surrender of pride, entitlement, and selfish ambition. It challenges us to examine our attitudes toward wealth, power, and privilege and to align our lives with the values of Jesus's kingdom.

Practical steps include:

- **Practicing gratitude.** Recognize that all we have is a gift from God, not a result of our own merit.
- **Serving with the marginalized.** Make a deliberate choice to become poor in spirit by caring for the poor, the weak, and the outcast in our communities.
- **Cultivating humility.** Engage in spiritual disciplines such as prayer, fasting, and confession as a way of resisting oppression, which remind us of our dependence on God.

When we live as the poor in spirit, we bear witness to the radical nature of God's kingdom—a kingdom where the humble are exalted, the last are made first, and the riches of grace are lavished on those who know they need it most.

Centering Thought

To be poor in spirit is to live in humility, acknowledging that all humans deserve nothing yet receive everything from God (Rom 3:12). It is to align our lives with Jesus, caring for the weak and vulnerable and embodying the values of God's kingdom.

Prayer

Jesus, make me like you!
Make me a humble servant who cares for the weak and poor,
living as a true citizen of your kingdom, already here and yet to come.

Personal Journal Prompts

- How do you think those close to you perceive you—as proud or humble?
- Do you believe you deserve more or less than what you have? Why?
- What practical steps can you take to care for someone who is weaker or poorer than you?
- In what ways does the example of Jesus challenge your understanding of humility and service?

Day 35

Justice

Scripture

Blessed are those who hunger and thirst for righteousness, for they will be filled.

—Matthew 5:6

He has told you, O mortal, what is good; and what does the Lord require of you but to do justice, and to love kindness, and to walk humbly with your God?

—Micah 6:8

The Necessity of Justice

JUSTICE IS ESSENTIAL FOR living in peace and achieving happiness. Injustice ignites anger even in the meekest among us. It is not merely an action but a pervasive reality—mindsets, environments, emotions, and intentions that deviate from God's love, manifesting in our behaviors and social, political, and religious systems.

Injustice is not just one thing; it is the accumulation of inequities that diminish human value repeatedly. At its core, injustice disintegrates the fundamental fabric of human existence: co-humanity and conviviality—the complementary and beneficial way of living in relation to others. The issue is not about achieving sameness; no one desires to be identical to another. Instead, it is about equitable access to opportunities and resources that enable a life of dignity.

When these opportunities and resources are limited by individuals or systems, we feel the weight of injustice—inequality and a devaluation of our humanity. Justice, then, becomes the necessary framework for ensuring that everyone can thrive according to their efforts but also their inherent worth as creatures of God.

God: The Source of Justice

God is just, and divine justice flows from God's love. Justice is one of the most defining characteristics of God, and it is inseparable from divine love. Because God loves, God is just. Because God is just, God loves. This divine cycle invites us to participate as instruments of justice in the world.

God's justice is active, constantly working to liberate the oppressed and restore peace. As followers of Jesus Christ, we are called to embody this justice in our personal lives and advocate for its presence in the public and private spheres. As the prophet Micah reminds us, the divine mandate is clear: "Do justice, and to love mercy, and to walk humbly with your God" (6:8).

Justice and the Cross of Christ

In the life and death of Jesus Christ, the stark reality of human injustice is laid bare. The crucifixion of Jesus—the ultimate act of injustice—reveals the depths of human capacity to judge, condemn, and devalue life itself. If such cruelty can be inflicted on the innocent and just Son of God, what horrors might befall others?

Yet, in the very injustice of the cross, we also see the justice of God at work. Jesus willingly bore humanity's injustice to open the door to salvation and the peace of God's kingdom. Through his death and resurrection, Jesus transforms the meaning of justice, showing that divine justice is not about retribution but restoration.

The church, as the body of Christ, is called to be a community of justice and peace. Its members are to act as instruments of justice, working to challenge systems of oppression and embodying the restorative justice of God in their relationships and actions.

Living as Instruments of Justice

Practicing justice begins with examining our own lives:

- Have we experienced injustice, and how have we responded?
- Have we been perpetrators of injustice, and if so, why?

Living justly requires humility, repentance, and a commitment to act in ways that align with God's kingdom values. It means not only seeking fairness in personal interactions but also advocating for systemic changes that address inequality and oppression.

Again, Glenn Stassen's *Kingdom Ethics* highlights the importance of active peacemaking as part of Jesus's vision for justice. True justice is not passive; it involves confronting systems of power that dehumanize and marginalize. It requires us to hunger and thirst for righteousness, continually seeking ways to live out God's love in tangible, transformative ways.

Justice Rooted in Love

Justice in the kingdom of God is inseparable from love. It is not merely about fairness but about restoring relationships and affirming the dignity of every person in their own context. In Jesus Christ, we see this justice in action:

- He welcomed the marginalized.
- He healed the sick.
- He confronted religious hypocrisy.

- He proclaimed good news to and with the poor.

To follow Jesus is to commit to a life of justice—a justice that liberates, heals, and reconciles. It is to hunger and thirst for righteousness, knowing that only in God's kingdom can true justice be found.

Centering Thought

Justice is the active work of restoring dignity, equity, and peace in a world marred by inequality and oppression. In Christ, we find the perfect example of a justice rooted in love, calling us to be instruments of God's justice in every aspect of our lives.

Prayer

Jesus, make me like you!
Make me a person who practices justice and works for peace,
living as an instrument of your kingdom.

Personal Journal Prompts

- Have you ever experienced injustice? How did it affect you, and what did you learn from the experience?
- Reflect on a time when you treated someone unfairly. What motivated your actions, and how can you seek reconciliation?
- How does the example of Jesus challenge your understanding of justice?
- In what ways can you work for justice in your community, workplace, or church?

Day 36

Peace

Scripture

Blessed are the peacemakers, for they will be called children of God.

—Matthew 5:9

*Peace I leave with you; my peace I give to you.
I do not give to you as the world gives.
Do not let your hearts be troubled, and do not let them be afraid.*

—John 14:27

The Necessity of Peace in a Fragmented World

To live in peace is to live joyfully. To practice peace is to work for the happiness of others. Anxiety creates restlessness, and restlessness breeds discord. Without peace, every relationship—no matter how close or affectionate—carries the latent potential for enmity. In hyperactive work environments and highly competitive societies, we often lose the ability to reflect on our social behavior. This loss fosters chronic anxiety, turning us into metaphorical "living grenades," primed to explode when our tolerance is exhausted.

These dynamics fuel interpersonal conflicts, leading to discord and irreparable losses. The resulting hostility compounds anxiety and stress, perpetuating a vicious cycle of conflict and fragmentation.

Peace as Divine Action

Peace is far more than an emotion or an ideal; it is the manifestation of divine harmony, God's sovereignty, and surrender to the Almighty. Without first receiving peace from the God of peace, we cannot authentically transmit it to others.

In Scripture, the Hebrew term *shalom* encompasses a profound vision of peace: wholeness, health, salvation, integration, trust in God, reconciliation, satisfaction, and lacking nothing. *Shalom* is a divine act that liberates victims and restores creation to its fullness. It is God's ongoing work in creation, gestating life and divine order from within chaos, shaping discord into harmony and brokenness into relational wholeness.

Jesus Christ: The Humanity of God's Peace

God's peace became incarnate in Jesus Christ. Through his life, death, and resurrection, the peace of God took on human form, becoming accessible and actionable in our nations, cities, communities, and families. Jesus Christ, as Emmanuel ("God with us"), offers his unique peace: "Peace I leave with you; my peace I give to you. I do not give to you as the world gives" (John 14:27).

The peace of Jesus is rooted in divine love poured into our hearts (Rom 5:5), a love that reconciles us with God and with one another. In Jesus Christ, we find the strength to bless those who harm us, pray for those who mistreat us, and even love our enemies. This radical practice of peace is impossible without Christ, for it is through him that we can replace discord with mercy and live free from anxiety and restlessness.

Peace in a World of Armed Conflict

In a time when more than fifty nations are embroiled in armed conflicts—the highest number since 1946[46]—peace is an urgent yet elusive reality. These wars reveal stark inequalities in who is deemed worthy of protection and who is considered disposable. In other words, those populations who are deemed more profitable are protected with the best war technology and world military support. Peace has been monetized!

From a decolonial perspective, peace must be reimagined as an act of justice and healing. Indigenous spiritualities often frame peace as a relational equilibrium with all beings, recognizing the interconnectedness of human, ecological, and spiritual realities. This wisdom teaches us that peace is not merely the absence of conflict but the presence of justice, dignity, and respect for all creation.

Jesus Christ embodies the kingdom vision of de-merchandizing life, standing in solidarity with the oppressed and dispossessed. His call to "love your enemies" and "pray for those who persecute you" (Matt 5:44) disrupts imperial logics of power and retribution. Instead, Christ invites us into a kingdom of reconciliation, where peace is practiced as restorative justice and communal healing.

Kingdom Ethics and the Practice of Peace

Glenn Stassen highlights this topic of peacemaking in *Kingdom Ethics*. He emphasizes that the Beatitudes are not passive virtues but active practices. To *work for peace* is to engage in transforming systems of violence and inequality into avenues for reconciliation and justice.

Stassen's "transforming initiatives" approach highlights actionable steps for living out Jesus's teachings:

- Address structural injustices that perpetuate poverty and violence.

- Engage in nonviolent resistance against oppression.

- Build communities of trust and mutual care that model the kingdom of God.

Cultivating Inner Peace

Behavioral psychology and emotionally healthy leadership suggests that peace begins with cultivating inner stability. Practices such as mindfulness, prayer, and community-support help regulate the anxiety and restlessness that undermine our capacity for peacemaking. The inner peace that comes from trusting in God's sovereignty empowers us to navigate conflict with grace and resolve.

Toward a Global *Shalom*

The practice of peace is not merely a personal endeavor but a communal and global responsibility. From the Hebrew prophets to Indigenous wisdom, the call for *shalom* is a call to create spaces where all can flourish. Jesus Christ, as the Prince of Peace, invites us into this sacred work:

- **In our families:** By addressing unresolved conflicts and fostering reconciliation.
- **In our communities:** By advocating for policies that protect the vulnerable and promote equity.
- **Globally:** By resisting militarism, supporting refugees, and amplifying the voices of the oppressed.

True peace, as Christ teaches, is an active pursuit of justice and restoration. It is the work of mending what is broken, standing with the marginalized, and embodying God's love in every interaction.

Centering Thought

Peace is both a divine gift and a sacred task. In Jesus Christ, we find the ultimate model of peace rooted in love, reconciliation, and justice. As peacemakers, we are called to embody this vision, transforming our homes, communities, and world into places where God's shalom reigns.

Prayer

Jesus, make me like you!
Make me a person who practices peace, even in the face of discord.
Help me to live as a peacemaker, bringing
your shalom to a fractured world.

Personal Journal Prompts

- How would you describe your current levels of stress and anxiety? What practices help you find peace in daily life?
- When you think of peace, harmony, and tranquility, what images or memories come to mind?
- How can you engage in peacemaking in your community, especially in addressing systemic injustices?
- What does it mean to you to practice the peace of Jesus in a world of conflict and inequality?

Day 37

Testimony
Auto-Historia as Spiritual Activism

Scripture

Blessed are you when people insult you, persecute you, and falsely say all kinds of evil against you because of me. Rejoice and be glad, because great is your reward in heaven.

—MATTHEW 5:11–12

The Necessity of Testimony

WE ALL NEED TO express our convictions to live authentically and joyfully. Repressing these convictions creates a dissonance that leads to unhappiness and a life devoid of integrity. When we are unable or unwilling to share our deeply held beliefs, or when external forces inhibit us, we experience a sense of imprisonment. Over time, suppressed convictions lose their vitality as the fire of passion and purpose that sustains them is extinguished.

Christian testimony, therefore, is not just an act of communication; it is the lifeline of conviction in the power of the Spirit. It keeps our faith alive and dynamic within ourselves while giving it visibility in the wider community. The Christian tradition upholds testimony as the public declaration of faith in the God who self-reveals through extraordinary acts in history and personal experience (*lo cotidiano*). To bear witness is to give voice to the God who has been made known to us, even in the face of opposition, misunderstanding, or persecution.

Testimony and the Cost of Authentic Witnessing

Testimony has always been a costly endeavor. In the Old Testament, prophets bore the burden of revealing God's justice and mercy, often at the expense of their safety and lives. In the New Testament, the call to be a witness to Jesus is extended to all his followers: "You will receive power when the Holy Spirit comes on you; and you will be my witnesses in Jerusalem, and in all Judea and Samaria, and to the ends of the earth" (Acts 1:8 NIV). This call is not merely an invitation to speak (a modern twist) but to embody the reality of God's reign in a world that often resists it.

Jesus Christ, as the ultimate revelation of God, is the faithful witness par excellence. His followers are tasked with being witnesses (martyrs) to the faithful witness. This involves belonging to Jesus's story by revealing the reality of God in everyday contexts through words, actions, and resilient faithfulness. However, the role of a witness carries an inevitable weight: the willingness to face suffering, marginalization, or persecution for the sake of Christ and his kingdom.

Belonging to Jesus's Story as the Basis for Testimony

Authentic Christian testimony does not arise from allegiance to patriotic narratives, political ideologies, or nostalgic traditions that idolize a "golden age" of Christianity. It is rooted in belonging to the story of Jesus—a story that critiques power, upends empires, and centers the marginalized. As Reinhold Niebuhr emphasized, the church must resist the temptation to align itself with dominant political forces and instead remain a prophetic voice that calls for justice, love, and reconciliation.⁴⁷

Walter Brueggemann's concept of *prophetic imagination* deepens this understanding, reminding us that Christian testimony challenges the "royal consciousness" of empire—a consciousness that normalizes injustice and suppresses dissent.⁴⁸ Testimony, then, becomes an act of resistance that reveals the alternative reality of God's kingdom—a world of justice, peace, and mutual care.

Testimony as Spiritual Activism: Learning from *Auto-Historia*

The concept of *auto-historia*, articulated by the Chicana intellectual Gloria Anzaldúa, enriches our understanding of testimony as a form of spiritual activism. *Auto-historia* is the practice of weaving personal narrative with collective memory, creating space and meaning for marginalized voices to reclaim agency and identity.⁴⁹ For Christians, *auto-historia* invites us to locate our testimony within the larger story of God's redemptive work in history and creation.

This approach challenges us to recognize how our personal stories intersect with systemic injustices and communal struggles. Testimony becomes an act of healing and resistance—healing the wounds of alienation and resisting narratives that dehumanize and exclude. Through *auto-historia* as testimony, we affirm that our lives are embedded in God's ongoing story, a story that holds the promise of restoration and renewal for all creation.

Living as Witnesses in a Fragmented World

In a world fractured by divisions—political, racial, economic, and religious—Christian testimony must embody reconciliation and hope. The Niebuhr brothers offer a framework for engaging these fractures with integrity. H. Richard Niebuhr's *Christ and Culture* challenges Christians to navigate the tension between faith and societal norms, while Reinhold Niebuhr's *Christian Realism* reminds us of the need for humility and perseverance in the face of systemic sin.

Testimony, therefore, is not about triumphalism or coercion but about vulnerability and solidarity. It calls us to walk alongside the marginalized, to speak truth to power, and to live in a way that reflects the love and justice of Jesus Christ.

The Cost and Joy of Testimony

Bearing witness to Jesus is not without cost. It may invite ridicule, isolation, or even persecution. Yet, it is also a source of profound joy and fulfillment. In Jesus, we find the strength to endure opposition and the grace to respond with love. His life, death, and resurrection model the ultimate testimony—a life given in love for the sake of the world.

Centering Thought

True testimony is not about defending ideologies or traditions; it is about embodying the story of Jesus in a way that reveals God's love and justice to a broken world. In our words and actions, we proclaim that another way is possible—a way of hope, reconciliation, and new life.

Prayer

Jesus, make me like you!
Make me a faithful witness to God's justice and mercy.
Help me to embody your story in a way that
reveals your kingdom to the world.

TESTIMONY

Personal Journal Prompts

- Have you ever experienced suffering or rejection because of your faith or pursuit of justice? How did you respond?
- How does belonging to the story of Jesus shape your understanding of testimony?
- Reflect on a time when your testimony—through words or actions—made a difference in someone else's life. What did you learn from that experience?
- What steps can you take to align your testimony with the values of God's kingdom, rather than the values of nationalistic power or privilege?
- How can you incorporate *auto-historia* into your testimony, weaving your personal story with God's redemptive work in the world?

Day 38

The Power of God

Scripture

The power of the Lord was with them, and a great number believed and turned to the Lord.

—Acts 11:21

Rethinking Power: From Control to Communion

WE ALL NEED THE power of God to live fully and to find true happiness. The opposite of God's power is not weakness or powerlessness but the distorted "power of man."[50] This power is the illusion of self-sufficiency and absolute control—the belief that human capabilities, imagination, and decisions can replace the divine. When we confuse the image of God within us with being God ourselves, we fall into a dangerous idolatry of self and end up stealing God's identity. That being the case, we may call our historical projects church, university, government, just war, or even ministry and mission, but in truth it is our "tower of Babel," as Barth puts it in chapter 1 of *Word of God and Word of Man*.[51] It is doomed to fail, sooner or later.

Humans are born with innate potential and capacities that, as we grow, we transform into personal power and influence. However, the belief that we can achieve unlimited power to control our lives and circumstances is a dangerous deception. Such a belief may inflate our egos for a time, but reality inevitably humbles us, revealing the truth of our fragility. We may appear as gods momentarily—through fame, wealth, and influence embedded in systems—but our humanity is eventually laid bare. We are fragile vessels, dependent on the Almighty.

Liberation Through Divine Power

The Christian tradition insists that the unlimited power of God can be experienced through faith, but this power originates in God alone. Paradoxically, to experience God's power, we must first acknowledge our weakness, vulnerability, and sinfulness. This recognition is not an admission of defeat but a step toward liberation. As feminist and liberation theologians emphasize, true power is not coercive but life-giving, capable of transforming systems of oppression and healing fractured relationships.

Sin, often understood as the misuse of human agency for selfish ends, enslaves us to cycles of harm and alienation. Genuine liberation begins when we acknowledge that we cannot free ourselves from these cycles by our own efforts. In Jesus Christ, God confronts and overcomes the powers of sin and evil, offering humanity the gift of redemption and renewal. God's power is limitless in its ability to liberate us from every human limitation and barrier, enabling our growth and flourishing in Christ's Spirit.

The Power of God in the Weakness of Christ

The power of God is the foundation of human redemption. We are not saved merely by personal merit or human strength but by the transformative power of God revealed in Jesus Christ, in the power of the Spirit. God became human in Jesus, embodying divine power in the vulnerability of human existence. Through his life, death, and resurrection, Jesus revealed that God's strength is made perfect in weakness (2 Cor 12:9).

Jesus's death, an act of ultimate vulnerability, displayed the paradoxical strength of divine love. His resurrection demonstrated that God's power is not about domination but about life-giving restoration. This power enables believers to live, not as dominators (Gen 11, tower of Babel) but as witnesses and servants (Acts 2, Pentecost). As Pentecostal theology reminds us, the Spirit of Pentecost empowers believers, not to control others but to live out the radical demands of God's kingdom marked by worshiping God through testimony, love, and service.

Power in Witness and Service

The power of God is not a tool for personal gain or domination but a resource for living out God's will and serving others. In the book of Acts, the disciples exemplify this power: Peter and John heal a beggar at the temple gate; Stephen boldly preaches forgiveness even as he is stoned; Priscilla and Aquila teach with wisdom and hospitality. These acts of power are not about ego but about embodying the resurrection life of Jesus Christ.

This understanding challenges "Babelian" patriarchal and colonial frameworks of power, which prioritize control and hierarchy at the service of extractionistic economies. Ecofeminist theologians emphasize that divine power is relational and nurturing, aligning with the rhythms of creation rather than exploiting them. Decolonial approaches likewise call us to reject the imperialist misuse of power that dehumanizes and exploits, inviting us instead to participate in the liberating power of God that restores dignity to the oppressed, enabling an ecology where all peoples fit and flourish. This is the ultimate eschatological vision of new creation.

The Power of God

The Paradox of Power in Weakness

To live in the power of God is to embrace the paradox of strength in weakness. Jesus's crucifixion, often dismissed as the ultimate failure, is in fact the supreme revelation of God's power—power that transforms death into life and enmity into reconciliation. Similarly, the apostle Paul teaches that God's grace is sufficient, and God's power is perfected in human weakness (2 Cor 12:9). This counters the modern obsession with self-sufficiency and control, reminding us that true strength comes from obedient communion with God and creation.

Power for Well-Living (*Suma Qamaña/Suma Kasay*)

The Indigenous concept of *Suma Qamaña* (Aymara) or *Suma Kasay* (Quechua), often translated as "well-living" or "living in harmony," offers profound insight into what this transformation entails. Rooted in communal wisdom and a deep connection with the land, well-living emphasizes balance, reciprocity, and the interconnectedness of all life. It challenges the dominant Western paradigm of "good life" through individualism, consumption, and competition. Instead, *well-living invites us into a relational mode of existence*, where flourishing is not measured by material accumulation but by the health of our relationships—with one another, with creation, and with the Creator.

God's Power as Reciprocity and Balance

The power of God, as seen through the lens of *Suma Kasay*, is not coercive or exploitative. It is a power that restores reciprocity and balance. Just as Indigenous communities understand the land as a living being deserving of care and respect, God's power calls us to steward creation with humility and responsibility. This divine power empowers communities to resist exploitation and to pursue right relationships that uphold the dignity of all beings.

In the Scriptures, this vision is reflected in Jesus's ministry, which consistently restores relationships and prioritizes the marginalized. His miracles often involve healing, feeding, and inclusion—acts that embody the principles of well-living. Jesus's life and resurrection show us that God's power is not about conquering but about renewing and reconciling.

Empowered to Resist and Flourish

Living in the power of God means embracing the call to resist systems of domination and exploitation. Ecofeminist theologians point out that these systems often harm both the Earth and its most vulnerable inhabitants, perpetuating cycles of violence. In contrast, God's power liberates us to live in ways that align with well-living, advocating for ecological sustainability, gender justice, and community flourishing.

Pentecostal theology underscores the role of the Spirit in equipping us for this mission. The Spirit does not empower us for self-aggrandizement (a distortion of prosperity gospel) but for service and witness, much like the first disciples in the book of Acts. This empowerment leads us to *belonging to Jesus's story* by embodying Christ's presence in the world as agents of healing and hope.

A Vision for Today

In a world marked by exploitation, inequality, and environmental degradation, the power of God as *Suma Kasay* offers a prophetic alternative. It invites us to imagine a society where well-living replaces exploitation, where cooperation replaces competition, and where harmony replaces domination. This vision aligns with the kingdom of God as preached by Jesus, where the last are first, the meek inherit the earth, and peace is not just a personal feeling but a systemic reality (the Beatitudes).

God's power calls us to *Buen Vivir*—not only for ourselves but for the entire web of life. To live in this power is to join in God's work of reconciliation and renewal, embracing our role as stewards of creation and partners in the flourishing of all beings.

Centering Thought

The power of God is not about control but communion, not domination but reciprocating liberation. In Jesus Christ, we witness a power that transforms weakness into strength and death into life. To live in this power is *Buen Vivir*, embracing humility, serving others, and participating in God's ongoing work of care, renewal, and justice of the web of life, Mother Earth.

Prayer

Jesus, make me like you!
Make me a person who embraces weakness to
Buen Vivir in the power of the Spirit.
Help me to be a vessel of your strength and a servant to my neighbors.

Personal Journal Prompts

- Do you see yourself as strong or weak? How does this perception affect your relationship with God?
- What aspects of your life might God be asking you to surrender as a sign of trust in his power? What are you pursuing, a good life or *Buen Vivir*? Ask around.
- Reflect on the disciples in Acts. How did they demonstrate God's power in their weaknesses?
- How can you use God's power to serve others and contribute to justice and healing in your community?

Day 39

Service as Christopraxis

Scripture

So if I, your Lord and Teacher, have washed your feet, you also ought to wash one another's feet. For I have set you an example, that you also should do as I have done to you. Very truly, I tell you, slaves are not greater than their master, nor are messengers greater than the one who sent them. If you know these things, you are blessed if you do them.

—John 13:14-17 NRSVue

The Transformative Power of Service

TRUE HAPPINESS DOES NOT exist apart from serving others. Yet, service is not all the same. Some serve only those they love; others serve those who can repay the favor. There are those who serve out of obligation, fearing loss of status or benefits, while others serve only themselves. Finally, there are those who go the extra mile, offering service to those who cannot repay them.

Service, at its core, is one of the most political activities of our lives. It often involves calculating the influence or benefit we might gain from our actions. What begins as seemingly noble or altruistic service can, over time, reveal ulterior motives. For many, the idea of selfless service may seem mythical, even impossible, as we assume every act hides some personal gain. Unfortunately, this mindset is not limited to secular contexts but is also found within Christian communities. Such self-serving approaches, even within churches, fail to reflect the essence of Christopraxis or Christ-shaped service.

Service as Obedience, Not Convenience

Christopraxis transforms acts of convenience into acts of commitment. The God of Scripture is merciful and generous, pouring blessings on the just and unjust alike. Similarly, Christian service is not transactional or tactical, waiting for the right moment to demand repayment. It is rooted in the conviction that we owe our neighbor kindness simply because God has designed us to live in mutual relationship. This also applies to the Earth, our most immediate neighbor.

In God's unfolding kingdom, service is an act of love—forgiving, caring for, challenging, and complementing others. The foundation of Christian faith is love for God and neighbor; the foundation of Christian living is service to both. To serve is to participate in the life of God's kingdom, where power is defined not by dominance but by humble acts of care and solidarity.

Jesus, the Servant of All

Jesus Christ is the ultimate servant, the fullest embodiment of sacrificial and joyful service. Through his incarnation, life, death, and resurrection, he models service from below that is rooted in love, humility, and obedience to God. When we follow Jesus, belonging to his story, we are transformed into servants, not out of obligation but out of love. To serve is to embody Christ's presence in the world.

Those who serve out of love for God become quietly influential, humbly powerful, and joyfully selfless. And, as Martin Luther King Jr. said, "Everyone can be great because everyone can serve." Service motivated by divine love transforms both the giver and the receiver, building communities of justice, compassion, and hope.

Insights from Service-Driven Movements

The Zapatista philosophy of *mandar obedeciendo*—"to lead by obeying"—offers a compelling framework for Christian service. In Zapatista communities, leaders are called to serve their people, listening to their needs and prioritizing communal well-being over personal gain. This approach resonates with the servant leadership of Jesus, who washed the feet of his disciples and laid down his life for others.

The Catholic Social Gospel emphasizes that service is not limited to charity but is a commitment to justice. It calls Christians to challenge oppressive systems while caring for the marginalized and vulnerable. Mother Teresa exemplified this by serving the "poorest of the poor," embodying Christ's love in her care for the sick, the dying, and the forgotten.

Similarly, Gandhi's philosophy of *ahimsa* (nonviolence) and his life of service remind us that true service is a form of resistance against injustice. Gandhi's dedication to serving others, particularly those oppressed by systemic inequalities, aligns with the gospel's call to love our enemies and work for reconciliation.

Movements like the "urban monks," inspired by monastic traditions, show us how to integrate service into daily life. By living in cities and committing to prayer, hospitality, and acts of mercy, they model a lifestyle that bridges faith and action, blending the contemplative and the active in service to others.

Power in Humble Service

To serve is to wield power differently. It is not power over others but power with and for others—a transformative power that nurtures relationships, promotes healing, and fosters justice. Service aligned with God's kingdom prioritizes the flourishing of all creation and reflects the divine mandate to love and care for our neighbors.

In African *ubuntu* collective philosophy, just as in other Indigenous traditions, service is often communal and interdependent. The health of the individual is tied to the health of the community and the land. Serving others is not a burden but a sacred responsibility that honors the interconnectedness of all life. This mirrors Jesus's teaching that "whoever wants to become great among you must be your servant" (Mark 10:43).

Centering Thought

True greatness and power lie in humble service. To serve others is to embody the love of Christ, transforming relationships and society through acts of mercy, justice, and compassionate imagination. In a world often driven by self-interest and power struggles, service rooted in God's love invites us to lead by obeying, to lift up the marginalized, and to honor the interconnectedness of all life.

Prayer

Jesus, make me like you!
Let me encounter you in each act of service.
Make me a servant motivated by your love,
willing to walk the extra mile,
and eager to serve those who cannot repay me.

Personal Journal Prompts

- Do you find it easier to serve others or to be served? Why?
- When you serve, do you expect recognition or repayment? How does praise and blame influence your actions?
- What practices of Jesus's service—washing feet, feeding the hungry, forgiving sins—most inspire you? How can you imitate them?
- How can the Zapatista philosophy of "leading by obeying," or Gandhi's vision of nonviolent service, transform your understanding of Christian leadership?

Day 40

The Last and Wretched of the World

Scripture

*Whoever becomes humble like this child
is the greatest in the kingdom of heaven. . . .
Take care that you do not despise one of these little ones;
for, I tell you, in heaven their angels continually see
the face of my Father in heaven.*

MATTHEW 18:4, 10

Embracing Humility and True Greatness

*Blessed are the little ones, the last, and the wretched of the world.
Blessed are those ignored by civilizing cultures,
the invisible ones, those who do not fit within the status quo,
because of their sickness, poverty, age, culture,
race, social class, gender, or [dis]ability—
Blessed are those who offer their low or high status to God.
These people are received by God and his angels as the great
and the first in the kingdom of heaven.*

WE WERE CREATED TO reach greatness and power through our humble relationship with God and God's creation. True human flourishing begins with voluntary humility before God and a humble attitude toward our neighbors, including Mother Earth. For some, life has been limited and reduced by external factors beyond their control. Let us not stay in complaint or lament forever. Instead, let us see our condition as an opportunity to surrender completely to God, transforming our struggles and poverty into gifts of humility before God. Let us remember, "God chose what is foolish in the world to shame the wise; God chose what is weak in the world to shame the strong" (1 Cor 1:27 NRSVue).

Others, however, may have experienced material abundance, social prominence, and privilege, placing them at the center of society and culture. Let us not be deceived by these comforts. The ultimate reality of human existence is a shared dependency on God's provision: "The rich will disappear like a flower in the field. For the sun rises with its scorching heat and withers the field; its flower falls, and its beauty perishes. It is the same way with the rich; in the midst of a busy life, they will wither away" (Jas 1:10–11 NRSVue).

Jesus Christ: The Model of True Greatness

Jesus Christ, the wealthiest, most powerful, and greatest being in the universe—the first and the last—came to earth to show us the way of true greatness. He voluntarily became the lowest, choosing humility even to the point of suffering humiliation and death on a cross. Many doubted his divinity because of this extreme humility. Yet this humiliation revealed his divine power. Only in Jesus can humanity find its true potential (*theosis*)—divinity in the form of self-emptying service.

For those who choose to become small and last for the sake of Christ, the reward is not worldly praise but intimacy with Jesus, who walks this path with us. This humility does not involve devaluing ourselves or others but instead leveraging our God-given value for God's purposes. It is, as some theologians describe, "leading with the head bowed down."[52] It reflects a confidence in our identity in Jesus that frees us from seeking affirmation through worldly metrics of success.

Learning from Jesus and the Little Ones

The life of Jesus is filled with profound examples of this humility. He washed the feet of his disciples, welcomed children, and dined with tax collectors and "sinners." In doing so, he demonstrated that God's kingdom belongs, not to the mighty but to those who embrace a childlike dependency on God. His actions show us that true greatness is found in making others feel seen, valued, and loved.

In other words, Jesus's embrace of children, the sick and [dis]abled, and the poor is not a gesture of pity but a declaration of their intrinsic worth and their unique contributions to the kingdom of God. These groups are often perceived through deficit-based models that emphasize what they lack rather than recognizing what they bring. Yet, Jesus teaches us that they offer dimensions of living that challenge our selfish, profit-driven, and fragmented selves, revealing aspects of God's kingdom that are otherwise obscured.

Children: The Gift of Wonder and Dependency

Children embody the spirit of curiosity, wonder, and vulnerability. Their openness to learning and their capacity for trust challenge adults who are often cynical, self-reliant, and wary of dependence. By calling us to become "like little children" (Matt 18:3), Jesus reminds us that entering God's kingdom requires a radical embrace of humility and dependency on God. Children teach us to slow down, delight in the present, and view life with wonder rather than calculated control. They strip us of our illusions of self-sufficiency, encouraging us to approach God with innocence and wholehearted trust.

[Dis]abled Populations: Witnesses to Interdependence

The [dis]abled[53] among us reveal the myth of individualism and remind us of the beauty of interdependence. In a society that prizes efficiency and productivity, [dis]ability challenges the idolatry of able-bodied perfection and exposes how much we need one another to flourish. Those with [dis]abilities enrich communities by disrupting normalcy with their resilience, empathy, and ability to foster creativity and patience. They call us to create spaces of accessibility, where every member is valued for who they are, not for what they "should" do. Their presence disrupts notions of worth tied to utility, echoing Jesus's kingdom ethic where the first shall be last, and the last shall be first (Matt 20:16).

The Poor: Teachers of Simplicity and Solidarity

The poor confront the insatiable greed and materialism that plague much of society. Living with less, they embody resilience and creativity in ways that often elude the wealthy. They remind us that true wealth lies in relationships, solidarity, and reliance on God rather than possessions. The poor expose the failures of systems that privilege the few at the expense of the many, and their witness calls us to radical generosity and systemic change. Their lived reality mirrors Jesus's own life of material simplicity and his preference for the marginalized as the bearers of God's kingdom promises (Luke 6:20).

Centering Thoughts

Each of these groups reveals the fractures in a society obsessed with profit, efficiency, and individualism. Children remind us to value wonder over control; [dis]abled populations show us the beauty of interdependence over independence; the poor teach us to prioritize relationships and shared humanity over wealth. Together, they challenge us to dismantle systems of power that exclude and exploit and to reimagine a community grounded in mutual care and humility.

By welcoming children, advocating for the [dis]abled, and centering the poor, Jesus demonstrated that these groups are not to be pitied or condescended to—they are to be learned from and celebrated. They embody values central to God's kingdom, values that call us to relinquish selfishness and strive for a more just and interconnected world. In their presence, we are confronted with our own poverty of spirit and invited to be transformed into more compassionate and whole individuals.

Prayer

Jesus, liberate me from the fiction of
worldly greatness, wealth, and privilege.
Jesus, make me like you!
Make me a little one in the world, and a great one in the kingdom!

Personal Journal Prompts

- Reflect on times when you felt belittled or invisible because of your circumstances or identity. How did these experiences shape your understanding of humility?
- Consider moments when you might have inadvertently belittled or dismissed others because of their social status, education, gender, culture, ability, or race. What motivated these actions, and how can you change this behavior?
- In what specific ways did Jesus demonstrate humility and solidarity with the marginalized in his life? How can you imitate his example in your daily relationships and actions?
- Think about what can you learn from children as well as impoverished and [dis]abled communities? Make a commitment to make life with them more often.

Epilogue
From Half-Way to All-the-Way Discipleship

THE JOURNEY OF THESE forty days has been a pilgrimage of transformation, beckoning you from the half-hearted discipleship that characterizes so much of modern faith to the radical, all-encompassing obedience exemplified by Jesus Christ. At its core, this journey is a call to follow Jesus, not in part but in full, surrendering not only our possessions and honors but the most difficult offering of all—our very selves. As Meister Eckhart observed, the second half of the way demands the complete renunciation of our will, aligning it entirely with the divine will.[54]

The Call to Obedience and Transformation

Obedience is not passive compliance but active alignment with God's purposes. It is the soil in which the seeds of discipleship grow into a flourishing witness of God's kingdom. To obey Jesus is to imitate him, not superficially but deeply, as a life shaped by the rhythms of surrender, humility, and love. This is not a transaction but a relationship of intimacy with the living Christ, who calls us into a life of ongoing transformation through the power of the Spirit.

The wisdom of the mystics and prophets across Christian history resonates with this truth. Thomas Kelly reminds us that when we fast from our own will to follow God's desires, the divine becomes manifest in us.[55] History bends toward renewal, and we become agents of God's purposes in the world. Liberation theologians echo this sentiment, urging us to recognize that obedience to Christ is a profoundly public act—a participation in God's liberating justice and love for the oppressed. It is through this obedience that personal and social change become possible.

A Journey of Spiritual Habits and Practices

Through these forty days, you have cultivated habits that align your heart, mind, and body with the life of Christ. Devotional reading, self-reflection, directed prayer, and Scripture meditation have deepened your awareness of God's presence and purposes. These practices are not an end in themselves but tools for living a life of ongoing discipleship. They have formed in you new patterns of thought, new desires, and new ways of being that belong to Jesus's story.

The journey has prepared you for more than individual transformation; it has equipped you to live as a witness to the kingdom of God in a fractured world. The humility, justice, and love cultivated in these practices are not private virtues but public testimonies, calling others into the same radical obedience that marks *the way of Jesus*.

From Days to a Lifetime of Discipleship

Forty days may have marked a significant season of renewal, but the work of discipleship continues. Imagine dedicating forty weeks, forty months, or forty years to Christopraxis. The years will pass, whether we are intentional with them or not. Why not let them pass in the pursuit of Christlikeness, building on the foundation laid during these days? This lifelong commitment mirrors the wisdom of an old hermit of desert Christianity called Brother John, who confessed to his disciples at his dying be, that *he taught nothing he had not first lived*.[56] This confession embodies the very character of discipleship.

Epilogue

Belonging to the Story of Jesus

True discipleship is not about supporting patriotic narratives, political ideologies, or nostalgic golden-age traditions of Christianity. It is about belonging to the story of Jesus—a story of humility, sacrifice, and decolonial love that reorients every aspect of our lives. Being the church of Jesus Christ in such a time as ours begins by remembering who we are and where we stand, namely, that our primary loyalty is to Christ, whose kingdom transcends and critiques all human structures of power and culture.[57] The church's prophetic imagination invites us to reject narratives of scarcity and domination, replacing them with God's vision of abundance and justice from the end of the Earth.[58]

The concept of *auto-historia*, as articulated by Gloria Anzaldúa, enriches this journey.[59] It invites us to see our life as part of the larger narrative of God's redeeming work in the world. Our testimony becomes a sacred story, woven into the fabric of God's greater story—a story that calls you to challenge systems of oppression, honor the image of God in every person, and live as a participant in God's unfolding kingdom of peace and justice.

An Invitation to Go All the Way

The invitation before you and me is clear: Do not stop halfway! Move forward, let us surrender our will entirely to the work of Christ in our midst (Christopraxis). Let us follow Jesus with a radical praxis: *decolonial love*. Let the virtues of humility, love, and obedience permeate every corner of our lives. Let the practices of devotion, reflection, and prayer continue to shape us together where we live (*lo cotidiano*). And let the power of the Spirit guide us as we walk the second half of the way—a journey that will lead us into the fullness of life in Christ. There is a God's *mañana* that must be planted today through the imitation of Jesus in such a time as ours.

A Closing Blessing

*May you be a disciple whose will is aligned with
God's will, even if you're not a Christian.
May you be a witness to Jesus in every word, deed, and silence.
May your life be a testimony of God's redeeming love,
and may you one day echo the words of Brother John:
"I never obeyed my own will but only God's,
and I never taught what I did not first live."
Jesus, make me like you!
Make me someone who walks all the way, in obedience,
humility, and decolonial love in a time of hatred.*

Rev. Dr. Oscar García-Johnson
Glendora, California
Advent 2024

Endnotes

1. Billy Graham Evangelistic Association, "Loneliness."
2. Thurman, *Strange Freedom*, 143.
3. E.g., Nouwen, *Way of the Heart*, 10–21.
4. Bonhoeffer, *Life Together*, xx.
5. This is a well-known Zapatista dictum.
6. See Fanon, *Black Skin, White Masks*, and hooks, *Teaching to Transgress*.
7. For example, see Friedrich Nietzsche's *Thus Spake Zarathustra: A Book for All and None*; and Ayn Rand's *The Fountainhead*.
8. Barth, *Word of God*.
9. Augustine, *Confessions* 7.12.18.
10. Horvath and Powell, "Contributory or Disruptive."
11. Gutiérrez, *Theology of Liberation*.
12. Scazzero, *Emotionally Healthy Leader*.
13. Nouwen, *Wounded Healer*.
14. Scazzero, *Emotionally Healthy Leader*.
15. Garcia-Johnson, *Spirit Outside the Gate*.
16. Scazzero, *Emotionally Healthy Spirituality*.
17. Gutiérrez, *Theology of Liberation*.
18. The term "colonial wound" was coined by Walter Mignolo and Rolando Vázquez, drawing heavily from concepts introduced by Franz Fanon. For example, see Fanon, *Black Skin, White Masks*, and Mignolo and Walsh, *On Decoloniality*.
19. Thurman, *Strange Freedom*.
20. Santos, *Epistemologies of the South*.
21. Santos, *Epistemologies of the South*.
22. Santos, *Epistemologies of the South*.

23. Balswick et al., *Reciprocating Self*.
24. Santos, *Epistemologies of the South*.
25. Kierkegaard, *Purity of Heart*.
26. Swan, *Forgotten Desert Mothers*, 102.
27. Wittgenstein, *Philosophical Investigations*.
28. Santos, *Epistemologies of the South*.
29. Barth, *Word of God*, 20.
30. Nouwen, *Wounded Healer*.
31. González, *Mañana*.
32. Vision of Humanity, "Highest Number."
33. Bonhoeffer, *Cost of Discipleship*.
34. Heschel, *Sabbath*.
35. Heschel, *Sabbath*, 22.
36. Nouwen, *Reaching Out*.
37. These are recurring concepts throughout Thomas Merton's writing. For example, see Merton, *Seeds of Contemplation*.
38. Heschel, *Sabbath*.
39. García-Johnson, *Embracing Fear*, 15–21.
40. Augustine, *Confessions*.
41. Augustine, *On the Trinity* 15.
42. Nouwen, *Wounded Healer*.
43. Bonhoeffer, *Cost of Discipleship*.
44. *Martyrdom of Polycarp* 9.
45. Stassen, *Kingdom Ethics*.
46. Vision of Humanity, "Highest Number."
47. Niebuhr, *Moral Man*.
48. Brueggemann, *Prophetic Imagination*.
49. Anzaldúa, *Light in the Dark*.
50. Barth, *Word of God*.
51. Barth, *Word of God*, 9–27.
52. Bekker, "Leading with the Head."
53. The bracketed "[dis]" serves as a protest against the assumption that this so-called disabled population lacks abilities. They possess different abilities but, like many of us, may lack some of the normalized competencies typically associated with the metropolitan individual.
54. Eckhart, quoted in Kelly, *Testament of Devotion*, 52.
55. Kelly, *Testament of Devotion*, 52.
56. Wortley, *Book of the Elders*, 10.

Endnotes

57. Niebuhr, *Moral Man*.
58. Brueggemann, *Prophetic Imagination*.
59. Anzaldúa, *Light in the Dark*.

Bibliography

Anderson, Ray S. *The Shape of Practical Theology: Empowering Ministry with Theological Praxis*. Downers Grove, IL: InterVarsity, 2001.

Anzaldúa, Gloria. *Borderlands/La Frontera: The New Mestiza*. San Francisco: Aunt Lute, 1987.

———. *Light in the Dark/Luz en lo Oscuro: Rewriting Identity, Spirituality, Reality*. Edited by Analouise Keating. Durham, NC: Duke University Press, 2015.

Augustine of Hippo. *Confessions*. Translated by Henry Chadwick. Oxford: Oxford University Press, 1991.

———. *On the Trinity*. https://www.newadvent.org/fathers/1301.htm.

Balswick, Jack O., et al. *The Reciprocating Self: Human Development in Theological Perspective*. Downers Grove, IL: IVP Academic, 2005.

Barth, Karl. *Evangelical Theology: An Introduction*. Translated by Grover Foley. Grand Rapids: Eerdmans, 1963.

———. *Word of God and Word of Man*. Boston: Pilgrim, 1928.

Bekker, Corné J. "Leading with the Head Bowed Down: Lessons in Leadership Humility from the Rule of St. Benedict of Nursia." *Inner Resources for Leaders* 3. www.regent.edu/journal/inner-resources-for-leaders/rule-of-st-benedict-12-steps-of-humility-in-leadership/.

Billy Graham Evangelistic Association. "Loneliness: Billy Graham Classic Sermon." *YouTube*, Aug. 7, 2023. https://www.youtube.com/watch?v=qjlVxZlDC6c.

Bonhoeffer, Dietrich. *The Cost of Discipleship*. Translated by R. H. Fuller. New York: Touchstone, 1995.

———. *Life Together: The Classic Exploration of Faith in Community*. New York: HarperOne, 1954.

Brueggemann, Walter. *The Prophetic Imagination*. Minneapolis: Fortress, 2001.

Camus, Albert. "Albert Camus—Banquet Speech." *The Nobel Prize*. https://www.nobelprize.org/prizes/literature/1957/camus/speech/.

Cone, James H. *The Cross and the Lynching Tree*. Maryknoll, NY: Orbis, 2011.

Bibliography

Deloria, Vine, Jr. *God Is Red: A Native View of Religion*. Golden, CO: Fulcrum, 2003.

Fanon, Frantz. *Black Skin, White Masks*. Translated by Charles Lam Markmann. New York: Grove, 2008.

———. *The Wretched of the Earth*. Translated by Richard Philcox. New York: Grove, 2004.

García-Johnson, Oscar. *Embracing Fear: Christian Re-Existence in the Trump Era*. Eugene, OR: Cascade, 2025.

———. *The Spirit Outside the Gate: Decolonial Pneumatologies of the American Global South*. Downers Grove, IL: IVP Academic, 2019.

García Márquez, Gabriel. *Love in the Time of Cholera*. 1st American ed. Translated by Edith Grossman. New York: Knopf, 1988.

González, Justo L. *Mañana: Christian Theology from a Hispanic Perspective*. Nashville: Abingdon, 1990.

Gutiérrez, Gustavo. *A Theology of Liberation: History, Politics, and Salvation*. Translated by Caridad Inda and John Eagleson. Maryknoll, NY: Orbis, 1988.

Heschel, Abraham Joshua. *The Sabbath*. New York: Farrar, Straus, and Giroux, 2005.

hooks, bell. *Teaching to Transgress: Education as the Practice of Freedom*. New York: Routledge, 1994.

Horvath, Aaron, and Water Powell. "Contributory or Disruptive: Do New Forms of Philanthropy Erode Democracy?" *Stanford Social Innovation Review*, Jan. 9, 2017. https://ssir.org/books/excerpts/entry/disruptive_philanthropy.

Jennings, Willie James. *After Whiteness: An Education in Belonging*. Grand Rapids: Eerdmans, 2020.

Kelly, Thomas R. *A Testament of Devotion*. New York: Harper & Brothers, 1941.

Kierkegaard, Søren. *Purity of Heart: Is to Will One Thing*. San Francisco: HarperOne, 2008.

Las Casas, Bartolomé de. *A Short Account of the Destruction of the Indies*. Translated by Nigel Griffin and Anthony Pagden. London: Penguin Classics, 1992.

The Martyrdom of Polycarp. https://www.newadvent.org/fathers/0102.htm.

Merton, Thomas. *Love and Living*. Edited by Naomi Burton Stone and Brother Patrick Hart. San Diego: Harcourt Brace Jovanovich, 1979.

———. *Seeds of Contemplation*. New York: New Directions, 1949.

Mignolo, Walter D., and Catherine E. Walsh. *On Decoloniality: Concepts, Analytics, Praxis*. Durham, NC: Duke University Press, 2018.

Moltmann, Jürgen. *God in Creation: A New Theology of Creation and the Spirit of God*. Translated by Margaret Kohl. Minneapolis: Fortress, 1993.

———. *Theology of Hope: On the Ground and the Implications of a Christian Eschatology*. Translated by James W. Leitch. Fortress, 1993.

Niebuhr, H. Richard. *Christ and Culture*. San Francisco: HarperOne, 2001.

BIBLIOGRAPHY

Niebuhr, Reinhold. *Christian Realism and Political Problems.* London: Faber & Faber, 1954.

———. *Moral Man and Immoral Society: A Study in Ethics and Politics.* Louisville: Westminster John Knox, 2021.

Nouwen, Henri J. M. *The Inner Voice of Love: A Journey Through Anguish to Freedom.* New York: Image, 1996.

———. *Reaching Out: The Three Movements of the Spiritual Life.* New York: Doubleday, 1975.

———. *The Way of the Heart: The Spirituality of the Desert Fathers and Mothers.* New York: HarperCollins, 2009.

———. *The Wounded Healer: Ministry in Contemporary Society.* New York: Image, 1979.

Österling, Anders. "Award Ceremony Speech." *The Nobel Prize.* https://www.nobelprize.org/prizes/literature/1957/ceremony-speech/.

Raheb, Mitri, and Mark A. Lamport, eds. *Emerging Theologies from the Global South.* Eugene, OR: Cascade, 2023.

Santos, Boaventura de Sousa. *Epistemologies of the South: Justice Against Epistemicide.* Boulder, CO: Paradigm, 2014.

Scazzero, Peter. *The Emotionally Healthy Leader: How Transforming Your Inner Life Will Deeply Transform Your Church, Team, and the World.* Grand Rapids: Zondervan, 2015.

———. *Emotionally Healthy Spirituality: Unleash a Revolution in Your Life in Christ.* Nashville: Thomas Nelson, 2006.

Stassen, Glen H., and David P. Gushee. *Kingdom Ethics: Following Jesus in Contemporary Context.* 2nd ed. Grand Rapids: Eerdmans, 2016.

Stein, David E. S. *The Contemporary Torah: A Gender-Sensitive Adaptation of the JPS Translation.* Philadelphia: Jewish Publication Society, 2006.

Swan, Laura. *The Forgotten Desert Mothers: Sayings, Lives, and Stories of Early Christian Women.* Mahwah, NJ: Paulist, 2001.

Thiong'o, Ngũgĩ wa. *Decolonising the Mind: The Politics of Language in African Literature.* London: Currey, 1986.

Thomas à Kempis. *The Imitation of Christ.* Translated by William C. Creasy. Notre Dame: Ave Maria, 1989.

Thurman, Howard. *Jesus and the Disinherited.* Boston: Beacon, 1949.

———. *A Strange Freedom: The Best of Howard Thurman on Religious Experience and Public Life.* Boston: Beacon, 1998.

Vision of Humanity. "Highest Number of Countries Engaged in Conflict Since World War II." June 11, 2024. https://www.visionofhumanity.org/highest-number-of-countries-engaged-in-conflict-since-world-war-ii/.

Walsh, Catherine E., and Walter D. Mignolo. *On Decoloniality: Concepts, Analytics, Praxis.* Durham, NC: Duke University Press, 2018.

Ward, Benedicta, trans. *The Desert Fathers: Sayings of the Early Christian Monks.* London: Penguin Classics, 2003.

BIBLIOGRAPHY

Wildman, Terry M., and First Nations Version Translation Council. *First Nations Version: An Indigenous Bible Translation of the New Testament.* Downers Grove, IL: InterVarsity, 2021.

Wittgenstein, Ludwig. *Philosophical Investigations.* Translated by G. E. M. Anscombe. New York: Macmillan, 1953.

Wortley, John. *The Book of the Elders: Sayings of the Desert Fathers: The Systematic Collection.* Cistercian Studies Series 240. Collegeville, MN: Liturgical, 2018.

www.ingramcontent.com/pod-product-compliance
Lightning Source LLC
Chambersburg PA
CBHW031356230426
43670CB00006B/562